CHASIN(

A Guide for the Newly Disabled

and for

Those Who Love Them

Blessings!

Dinah

By

Dinah Chaudoir Federer

Chasing Normal

**A Guide for the Newly Disabled
and for
Those Who Love Them**

ISBN: 978-0-615-26262-8

Published by Distynct Solutions, LLC, Holland, OH 43528

Printed by McNaughton-Gunn, Saline, MI 48176

Cover Concept by Don Federer
Cover Design by Kevin Kennedy

This book is dedicated to my husband Don.

His love and support have been unfailing.

ACKNOWLEDGEMENTS

So much time, blood, sweat, and tears go into writing a book. It's difficult to thank everyone who has impacted the process. Of course, my first heartfelt thanks has to go to my husband. Don has been with me, not just through the writing of the book, but also through the trials and tribulations associated with a new disability. He is a gentle tower of strength, faith, and love. He is a gift in my life.

My family taught me to be independent as a child by not treating me differently. For this I am grateful. To my father Rod, you kept me safe and encouraged independence at the same time. Your support and love were a marvelous balancing act that I will be in awe of for as long as I live. How lucky I am to be your daughter. To my mother Lynn, my stepmother Judy, my brothers Tom, Dan, and John, thanks for your expectations of me. I am strong and happy because you expected nothing less.

Thank you to Carol for all the typing and support as we wrote our books together. You helped make the entire process so much less painful. Thanks also to Joyce, Bev and Karen for your eagle eye when proof reading the manuscript. And thank you Arionnah for your encouragement through the process.

Nancy R., Dan H., JoKasha, Mary T., Jean C., Amean, Saeid and Marina, you have taught me so much about healing the body, mind and spirit! Thank you for sharing your work with the world.

Thank you to Chrissy Ogden Marsh for allowing your fabulous artwork to be a part of this project. Your work is a gift to all of us.

Finally, thank you to my friends, colleagues, and clients who have taught me so much over the years.

CONTENTS

We can do no great things —
only small things with great
Love.

Mother Teresa

We are all travellers in the wilderness of
this world, and the best that we can find
in our travels is an honest friend.

Robert Louis Stevenson

Those who want to sing
will find a song.

Chasing Normal

Prelude

When I graduated from high school, the keynote speaker said something like, "By tomorrow you'll only remember 80% of what I say today. Within a week you'll only remember 50% of what I said." And, he predicted that in a very short time we'd remember less than 10% of what he said. Well, that prediction is the *only* thing I remember from his speech. So, given our capacity to be overloaded by life, I'm suggesting, both at the beginning and at the end of this book, what you may want to REMEMBER.....

THINGS TO REMEMBER
AS YOU GO THROUGH YOUR JOURNEY.....

- Be kind to yourself
- Look for reasons to celebrate what you've done and what you're doing
- Talk about "IT"
- Ask for help
- Feed your Spirit
- Take a nap
- Be open to doing things differently than before
- Plan ahead and be safe
- Meditate, relax
- Get out and give back
- Trust in higher wisdom; look for the learning and teaching opportunities
- Be patient with yourself and with loved ones; you're all learning a new way of life
- There is wisdom in taking it "one day at a time"
- Pay attention to what you eat
- Exercise

For so long now the need to write about the issue of disability and the feelings that go with it has been hammering at me. Where should I start? Who do I think I am anyway? I'm not a doctor. Do I have the right to say anything at all?

So let's address the first big question. "Who am I to write about disability?" I am a disabled adult. I was born with a mobility impairment. I use crutches or a scooter to get around. I also developed trigeminal neuralgia at age 35. It's horrific nerve pain that comes and goes without warning.

I'm also a vocational rehabilitation counselor. I help people with disabilities move into employment. I've worked in the field of rehabilitation for almost 20 years. I used to tell my newly disabled clients that my experience was vastly different from theirs because I grew up with my disability. I didn't have that sudden shock and adjustment that the newly disabled have to face. That chasm between my experience and that of the newly disabled was bridged by the trigeminal neuralgia. I am now someone who has experience on both sides. I grew up with a disability, and I've experienced the terror that goes with the sudden onset of a disability. I guess I'm a triple agent since I've experienced disability from three sides, the disability I was born with, the disability I acquired, and the disabilities that my clients and I address together.

Blessed is the influence of one
true, loving human soul on another.

george Eliot

Chapter 1

My Story

I belonged to a small writers' group. Our goal was to help each other bring our writing ideas to life. At one gathering, my friend was wondering whether or not she should include her personal experience with the issue she was writing about. My advice to her was, "Absolutely! Your experience is what gives you credibility!" After our meeting, I started thinking that perhaps I should take my own advice and share something with you about my personal journey through disability. So, here's my story......

I'm 42 years old as I write this. I've been dealing with my primary disability of Charcot-Marie-Tooth (CMT) since birth. This is an inherited neurological condition that affects the nerves and weakens the muscles in the extremities. I was very ill as an infant. I'm told I had pneumonia five times before I was one year old. I didn't walk until I was about five years old. To this day, I've never been able to walk independently. I've always needed to walk along the wall, grab furniture along the way, hold onto someone's arm, or use crutches.

My brother has told me that the doctors suggested my parents institutionalize me. In the 1960's, there were no early intervention programs to help disabled babies. Parents of disabled babies had to choose between giving their baby up to an institution or going it alone. Fortunately for me, my parents kept me, and I was encouraged to be as "normal" as possible.

Throughout my early years, I was very fortunate in that there were caring adults who watched over me. Recently, my dad told me that the doctors wanted to do exploratory surgery on me as an infant. They wanted to operate to find out why I kept getting pneumonia.

My dad's boss was an angel in disguise. She said, "You're only going to have the best if you're going through with this." She flew in a specialist from another city.

That doctor spent an hour with me in a room the day before he was planning to operate. No one else was allowed in. After examining me, he told my parents that I didn't need surgery. He said that my muscles, including my swallowing muscles, were weak from being ill. They were feeding me lying down as they do with all babies, but that caused the formula to enter my lungs which caused the pneumonia. He told them to feed me sitting up which would strengthen my swallowing muscles and prevent further illness. I was spared the surgery because of the concern and kindness of my dad's boss. One person really can make a difference in the lives of others.

When I was young, there were no physical therapists to come to the home as there are today. Luckily, my Dad is an engineer and an inventor. He created things to encourage me to walk. Our dining room had a sheet of plywood with pipes around the outside and the middle of the board. When I walked around the board, I could hold onto the pipes on either side of me and walk around the board. It was my "walking board" and I was supposed to practice on it daily. It never seemed like therapy to me. I felt like I had a jungle gym in the house – lucky me!

My dad created lots of therapeutic toys. Because of him, I did learn to walk. I also had three older brothers who would sometimes play walking games with me. I remember them holding onto my hands and walking me through the house in a fun way that was also therapeutic.

I was enrolled in school at the proper age and did fine. Of course, I endured the teasing and name calling that any child who is different has to journey through. I remember asking my Mom why I had to be disabled. I reminded her that everyone else in the family was fine. Why me?

My mom then shared a bit of wisdom that has carried me through some pretty hard times. She said "Dinah, just because you can't see their disability doesn't mean they don't have one. Everyone in the world has something that they have to deal with. Maybe it's a weight problem, maybe self esteem, perhaps a learning disability. Everyone has challenges whether you know about them or not." What a wise observation.

I knew in my heart that she was right. With that bit of wisdom to lean on, I never felt that I had the right to feel sorry for myself. In fact, it made me want to try to help others feel better about themselves. I knew very early that I would go into a helping profession.

It was always expected that I would go to college. My dad believed in education and in work. He always said "Never allow yourself to be dependent on a man. You have to always be able to support yourself" – great advice!

I did go to college. This was before the Americans with Disabilities Act (ADA) brought accessibility issues to light. Schools were not expected to accommodate disabled students as they are now.

I remember calling one of the largest University campuses in the state. They were known for being very progressive and I wanted to go there. I told them that I had a mobility impairment and I asked them if they provided assistance to students with disabilities. The answer I received was something like, "Well, you'll make friends when you get here and I'm sure someone will help you." That was far from comforting when you factor in a huge campus and some snow storms! I was hoping for a disabled students' transit system, since I was quite sure I wasn't the only disabled college bound student. Society's expectations hadn't caught up to mine at that point.

Finding schools that were accessible was tough, but my dad figured it out again. He found a small private school that I could physically negotiate and off I went. I didn't have the variety of courses and majors that the university provided but I did have a campus that was small enough that I could walk where ever I needed to go.

I have a BA in psychology and a minor in sociology. I was about 22 when I graduated from college. Like most young people, I was sick of school and couldn't wait to find a job. It took me over a year to find a full-time job. In the meantime, I worked part time at a youth center. At the end of my first year with the youth center, I was told that they weren't going to renew my contract. I was being released. The director told me that too many things had been broken by the kids when I worked. He said that, in his opinion, my disability prevented me from watching the kids closely enough.

It's important to note that, most of the kids using the Center, were "at risk" youth. They didn't have stable home lives and were often having problems at school too. The Center kept them off of the street and out of trouble. I didn't think a broken pool cue every now and then was a huge deal. The kids listened fairly well and enjoyed themselves and that was what mattered to me.

I considered a discrimination suit, and found a lawyer who would take my case. My father, a very wise businessman, said it would be a huge mistake. Again, this was before the ADA. Rights for people with disabilities were not really a "given." His concern was that in a small town, I'd be branded a trouble maker and finding a job would then be impossible. I didn't sue. I kept interviewing. It was horribly stressful to be a recent college graduate with no experience AND have a disability. It got to the point that I'd vomit after interviews. Finally, I was hired as a case manager at a rehab center for adults with cognitive disabilities and/or mental illness. The job came along just before my other contract ended.

I worked at the rehab center for four years. I continued to interview for other jobs. I actually had one interviewer say to me, "I like your philosophy and approach to rehab, but your disability makes you a liability, and I can't take that risk." It infuriated me. But I was young. I had no idea what to say. Ignorance and fear are hard to confront. I said nothing to him. I just left the interview shocked that someone would actually say that.

In time, I was hired by the State as a Vocational Rehabilitation Counselor. I help people with disabilities become employed. I've been doing this type of work for 17 years. I love what I do because I believe that moving toward independence and self-sufficiency puts people back on their own path - the path that they had to deviate from because of their disability.

I was probably unable to fully comprehend how far off center a *new* disability can throw a person before I had to deal with my own new disability. From my own experience, growing up with a disability is a completely different experience than *acquiring* a disability. I was 35 when I was diagnosed with trigeminal neuralgia. It causes intense electrical shock-type pain in the nose, lips and eyes. In my opinion it is pure torture and horribly anxiety provoking. The medication for it has significantly changed my way of life. It has made me much weaker. I'm no longer able to manage steps or walk very far. I fall more and rarely go places alone.

This was a bitter pill to swallow. I had always prided myself on being active and independent. Now I'm so tired at the end of the work day that I do little else. I am not nearly as active as I was before. This is not the plan I had for my life. Remember that I spent my life being as "normal" as possible. I worked, cooked and cleaned (badly), did laundry, shopped and socialized with friends.

While I certainly am not claiming I did everything single handedly in my everyday activities, I am saying I contributed. My husband has quietly and graciously picked up the slack as my stamina has decreased. He would never say an unkind word about my decreased level of contribution. He has never complained. However, I have never had his wisdom or his grace! I do get irritated. I do become frustrated. I do feel fear. This acquired pain syndrome makes my mobility impairment seem like a cake walk. It has made me stop comparing myself to that nebulous "normal" that I once felt so close to. It has brought me a first-hand understanding of anxiety, because each bout of pain brings waves of terror with it. I never know how severe it will get, how long it will last, or if I'll end up in the emergency room begging for help. It has made me release my own need to control.

It has, like any other acquired disability, permanently changed my life and my world. It has become my teacher, and I have become the reluctant student. I see that very real relationship on my good days – the not so good days are too full of survival techniques that just help me get from minute to minute for me to care about this change in my life.

This new disability has taught me more about compassion for others and for myself. It has taught me to trust more in an individual's own knowledge of his/her body and limitations and strengths. It has helped me to understand that pain can't always be ignored. Sometimes pain is going to be calling the shots. It has taught me that I need to pay attention more.

My opportunity in this crisis has been very real. It has opened my heart. Prior to my health "crisis," I approached difficult situations with a "bite-the-bullet" (as my dad would say) attitude. I personally plowed through much of my life by thinking I needed to ignore discomfort or fatigue and keep chasing "normal." I would become impatient when others didn't do the same. That's because I didn't understand true pain – I had never experienced it.

Well, thanks to trigeminal neuralgia, I get it now. I know what pain does to one's quality of life, to one's interest in life. When my trigeminal pain is actively spasming, it hurts to eat, to brush my teeth; even drinking water can trigger it. There have been times when all I can do is exist because the pain is unbearable. Now I know that, for people in pain, just getting through the day can be an incredible accomplishment. Now I can approach people in pain with love and an open heart. I can be with them without judgment.

I've learned to respect people's decisions on their treatment. I tried every natural alternative thing I could find because I was determined to heal myself naturally. Reiki, other hands-on healing, herbs – nothing worked for me. I still believe in natural healing, but I chose to go with a conventional medical treatment called gamma knife surgery.

Enter judgment! I beat myself up for a long time because I didn't succeed in using the power of my mind to heal my body. I felt like a failure. So couple guilt and failure with fear and anxiety about the procedure, and you have one exhausted, conflicted woman.

The gamma procedure shoots radiation at the nerve, next to the brain stem to kill it. I had it done to both sides and I have exposed myself to two hours of radiation now. When I tried to taper down on my medication, the pain came back and was persistent for three months, even when I returned to my regular dosage of medication. The pain is a bit less daunting in intensity since the Gamma procedure, but I am still horribly disappointed that it didn't completely free me from pain.

Now I read a lot to keep my mind off "What if?" Before, all my reading was focused on how to heal and how to move through physical issues by developing spiritually. I do believe it helped me but not in the way I had hoped. Now I'm taking a breather and reading mindless fiction that simply entertains me. Nora Roberts' trilogies have kept me entertained for hours. And, God bless the Harry Potter series! I'm grateful for the escape into fiction. That helps in its own way too. It takes me elsewhere and helps me relax.

During all of this, my husband has been a godsend. He has been and continues to be patient with the person I've become – someone who can be tender and more compassionate, as well as someone who is tired all the time, and very sedentary. Some people in my life have been understanding. Some have joked; some just stay away. They don't understand that when I constantly decline offers, it's because I can't physically muster energy I don't have. Occasionally, I get to experience others seeing me as having given up or given in. It's the same judgment I once dished out so freely. Life is a circle.

I work 40 plus hours per week and exercise at lunch three times per week. I haven't given in. I'm managing what I have. And, I can honestly say that I'm okay with however other people need to see me. Doing the best I can each day is enough for me. I no longer feel that I know the divine plan for my life. At first, I felt God had betrayed me by giving me another disability. Then, one day a co-worker, who was battling bladder cancer, said of his own challenge, "Hey, my life didn't come with guarantees for a certain number of years. I've had a good life, and we'll see what happens next." That struck me as wisdom I needed to adopt. My life didn't come with any guarantees

20

either, so I can't be mad at God. I just have to see what happens next.

I used to have a card that had a Chinese character on it. The card said that the character used for crisis is the same as the one used for opportunity because there is opportunity in every crisis. I lost the card years ago, but I still try to remind myself of this and share my belief in its message with my clients.

So that's where I am now. I'm nicer to myself and others. I work hard to help others toward their own healing path because I know it exists for all of us. I believe that life with a new disability is more challenging, but it really doesn't have to suck, which is exactly what I say to my clients. I believe that part of my purpose in life is to help others believe that too. This is why I'm taking the time to write this book. I believe that we, the disabled, need to stop chasing normal, celebrate who we are and who we are becoming, and help each other as we go.

I guess we'll see where our journey together takes us. There is so much about disability to discuss because, if you're newly disabled, or you love someone who is, you probably have millions of questions. I'll do my best to address what I can. For now, my best advice is to breathe deeply and hang on.

I am an idealist. I don't know
where I'm going, but I'm on the way.

Carl Sandburg

Chapter 2

Describing Blue

Let me tell you a story......

When I was in grade school, the school I attended had a separate classroom for kids who were blind or visually impaired. They were "mainstreamed" or integrated into as many regular education classes as possible. I always volunteered to go get those students when it was time for them to join our class. I was fascinated by Braille and really liked being with them.

One day we were having a Halloween party. I was sitting next to John, one of the blind students. I started describing things to him so that he would feel a part of what was going on. In describing one of the kid's costumes I told John that her mask was blue. At that point, I stopped and asked him if he knew what blue was, because it occurred to my nine year old mind that color may not be an understandable concept to him. John said he lost his sight at age two, and he thought he remembered some colors. So I tried to describe blue. "Blue is the color of the sky and the lake," I said to him. I think I quit the topic of blue at that point.

Although I wouldn't have been able to adequately articulate my realization then, the "aha" of that experience always stayed with me. Reviewing it as an adult made me realize that when I understood that he may not have actually seen the color blue, I needed to describe the "experience" of blue. Even as I did that, I realized that it still may not be making sense to him. Did he even have a memory of seeing the sky or the lake? So back then I did what any kid would have done; I moved on to another subject.

This story or memory has become an important touchstone in my life and my work. When I'm trying to discuss a topic with someone and I realize they have no frame of reference, I think to myself "Okay, this is like describing blue." Basically, you either know what blue is or you don't. I can't make you know blue. However, I can give you enough information about it so that, when you see it, you can hopefully recognize it.

And so it is with disability. You may not have first-hand experience with what I'm telling you. But maybe what I have to share with you will help you recognize important markers and road signs along your own journey.

So, let's begin to describe blue (or what it's like to be disabled) – shall we?

When I meet with a newly disabled person for the first time, I always try to ask them how they're doing, and how they're coping with life. The responses obviously vary. Many will simply say they're fine – more out of habit than anything else. I usually push them by making a statement like this:

"If you feel angry, scared, nervous, depressed, if you're avoiding your friends because you feel like all you do is complain, if you're crabby and snapping at your family—if you are doing any or all of these things, I can tell you that you're completely normal and it's okay. I can tell you that becoming disabled is like having the door slammed on your old life. It's terrifying. I can also tell you that new doors do open. **There is life after disability, and it doesn't have to suck.**"

That statement has opened the proverbial flood gates for many newly disabled people because it's the first time they've heard it. By the time they weave their way through a mind-numbing maze of doctors, nurses, and therapists for the treatment of their injury and related pain, the psychiatrist for "situational depression," and maybe an attorney or two to address the legalities of the injury, they're exhausted.

Our society is so fond of specialization. Each professional has addressed his/her piece of the puzzle (the problem they're helping the disabled person deal with), and then the individual with the disability is pushed down the conveyor belt to the next professional. Unfortunately, the pitfall with specialization is that there is a presumption that the next stop on the treatment assembly line will address whatever was missed at the one before. That doesn't often happen.

If you, as a newly disabled person, haven't yet talked with someone about how you **feel**, it might be time to do just that. My suggestion is that you find a qualified therapist who is comfortable with, and specializes in grief counseling. Grieving the loss of functioning is not that different from grieving the loss of a loved one. You need someone to help you move through feelings of grief and loss that are very normal.

When talking to my clients, I often give them a mini lecture about taking charge of their health care and their recovery. Doctors and lawyers are people first. And, like the rest of the population, there are good ones and not-so-good ones. Rather than putting these professionals on a pedestal, and then following them without question as a child follows a parent, I suggest people take on the role of manager to actively manage their recovery.

It is my opinion that doctors and lawyers are our "employees." We are **paying** them to provide a service. Like any good employee, they get to keep their job as long as they continue to provide quality service. If the quality starts to slip, we should as good managers, bring that to their attention. If, after that, they continue to avoid our questions and concerns and don't return our calls and cut our time short etc., **fire them**. No responsible manager would continue to employ someone whose performance is consistently substandard. Remember to maintain this role of manager as you search for another professional. At your first visit, interview them. Tell them what you expect, and see how they react to the job requirements. Trust your gut instincts in making your decision.

Some will be critical of my advice and say I'm promoting doctor hopping. I'm not doing that at all. I believe that no one has to tolerate poor service, and to some, that's an enlightening and empowering concept. I feel differently than most because I grew up with doctors poking, prodding, and testing me because no one could figure out what I had. Because I didn't walk until the age of five, many of them presumed that I was cognitively disabled. This was highly offensive to me and still is because this type of presumption still happens occasionally.

About ten years ago, I went to see a neurosurgeon based on my neurologist's referral. I was considering having a nerve biopsy done. This man had a good reputation, but my initial impression was that he was more than a bit arrogant. As the appointment progressed, my husband asked if taking the nerve sample from the side of my right foot would affect my driving because my foot would be permanently numb where they removed the nerve. The doctor laughed and said, "Well, since I don't think women should drive anyway, I'm not concerned."

I knew he was making a 'good ol' boy' joke for my husband

(who didn't find it amusing). Obviously, this doctor had no clue how his comment would affect me, the prospective patient. I was furious. I said something like: "At this moment I'm the one making the payment on your BMW and your condo in Florida. So, since you're on my dime I would appreciate a serious response to the question asked!" He then looked at me and actually said, "Now don't you get snippy with me Young Lady."

Anyone who thinks it's acceptable to make sexist jokes and take a condescending and paternalistic tone with me, doesn't get to work for me. If a doctor is disrespectful to my face, why would I trust him to do good work when I'm under anesthesia? Reputation or not, I would never allow that doctor to touch me. I wouldn't have cared if he had a recommendation from the President of the United States. If a doctor doesn't take his time with me seriously, he doesn't get hired. Or, if we're already working together and his performance deteriorates, I can fire him. That's how corporations flourish. Why would we be any less proactive with our bodies?

Another part of managing your healthcare/recovery is to keep good records. Get a notebook and take notes during every doctor or attorney visit. Be sure to include the date of the discussion and the important topics covered. If the doctor fills out any forms for work or for the insurance company, be sure to get a copy for your own records.

If you have a work related injury, contact the main Worker's Compensation Office (probably in your state capital) and ask them for information on the worker's comp process and what your rights and responsibilities are under the law. You need to become your own informed advocate because it's all quite complicated. But stay calm and take it one step at a time.

Whatever the cause of your situation, if you can't return to work for an extended period of time, you might want to explore whether or not Social Security benefits are right for you. This is a lengthy process for many, and may involve several rejections by Social Security and subsequent appeals on your part. It's important to stay on top of this. If you get a rejection, act on it immediately. If you toss it aside and forget to follow through, you may lose the right to appeal and/or to reapply for a significant period of time.

This is a lot to think about when you're already overwhelmed by the disability itself. Remember that we human beings are resilient. Ask for help when you need it, and take a nap when you need to replenish your energy.

I've often said to my clients that being newly disabled is like being dropped in a foreign country without a map. You're left with your own survival skills to try to find your way back home. We've only briefly touched on the medical and legal realms. What about returning to work? Can you do your old job? Do you have to find a new job? How does your spouse get an understanding of what you're going through? How do you explain it to your kids? What do you do if you can't do your old hobbies? The list of questions is endless because adjusting to a new disability is unique to the individual.

Something many of us have in common, however, is that nagging voice in our heads that judges what we do as inferior to how we would have done it prior to our disability. It's the "inner critic." Have you ever heard a movie critic trash a movie you loved? Do you remember dismissing his/her statements as untrue or poorly presented? Well, that's what you need to do with the "inner critic"— disregard it completely.

My first suggestion is to tell your inner critic to back off and be quiet. Resist the urge to listen to that voice in your head that says, "You used to be able to lift that!" "You should be able to walk that far." "You used to be able to _____."

If the measuring stick is always based upon your pre-injury or pre-disability lifestyle, how are you helping yourself? Using that criteria you'll never feel good about who you are today, and today is all that matters. So, when that internal critic wants you to critique what you can't do, remind yourself that you're surviving, and that you're teaching yourself how to **thrive** in a new world. Keep telling yourself, "I'm doing fine. Today is all that matters."

As weird as this may sound to you, consciously celebrate each accomplishment with yourself and anyone who is significant in your life—the first time you walk to the living room, the first time you use a teaspoon and feed yourself, the first time you _____. Celebrate each first. Yes! Before, in your old life, these activities may have been routine. But you're creating a new life now. Maintaining an attitude of celebration and gratitude, even for the little things, can help you remain open and receptive to continued healing.

When I was diagnosed with trigeminal neuralgia, I had a horrendous attack of pain that landed me in the emergency room, begging for relief. By the time the medication started to calm the pain, I couldn't walk. Because of my pre-existing mobility impairment, I found out certain meds make me too weak to walk. I could only take a few steps if someone was holding onto me with a gait belt. I was off of work for a month and terrified that my situation might not improve.

The doctor wouldn't believe it was medication related. I told him I knew my body, and I was well aware of cause and effect within my own body. Actually, frustration and sarcasm took over and I believe I said something like: "Hmmm, I could walk before and then I took the medication you prescribed. After taking the medication I couldn't walk. There seems to be a cause and effect relationship here!" I demanded a different medication, and slowly my strength returned. I remember feeling immensely proud of myself the first time I stood long enough to make instant pudding for dinner. It sounds small, but it meant the world to me. Be proud of all that you do.

Asking for help when you need it is another huge but necessary adjustment so you don't exhaust yourself. It seems this is a difficult thing for the non-disabled in general. I've seen my clients feel completely devastated by having to ask someone to help them, even family members.

Since I grew up walking with crutches, I was used to asking for help often. I was surprised to find that this was so hard for people who were adjusting to disability. It didn't take me long to understand that, of course, it's hard because it makes the disability more real. It hurts the ego to say "I can't." It hurts the heart and soul to say "I can't because this is real."

When I discuss this with my clients, they often cry. Their tears, I believe, are from exhaustion. They're spending all of their energy and often exacerbating pain levels by trying to pretend they're fine, or that they're the "same as before" their injury or diagnosis. They never sat down with their spouse and kids and said, "I need your help!" Most families respond well; they usually rise to the challenge when they understand what is needed. Many of my clients have told me that their kids handle it very well once they're informed of the real situation, and what they need to do to pitch in.

Children need to understand that when Dad asks them to take out the garbage or Mom needs them to do the dishes, it's because their help is truly needed. It's not just about contributing to household responsibilities as before. Kids respond to being needed. —I'm not advocating that kids become your personal assistants. They need to be allowed to be kids too. I'm saying that letting them know you need help keeps things honest.

I think it's important for me to say that, in my opinion, adjusting to and becoming comfortable with a disability is a life long process, as is any goal that relates to human character. Family discussions will need to be held periodically as things change so that everyone understands what's happening and can adjust accordingly.

It's like that classic goal of "being happy." How many times have we all heard people say: "I'll be happy when I have more money or a better job or a better relationship"? These things don't give us happiness on a platter. Happiness comes from within, whether you have these things or not. Happiness is relative as we move up and down the spectrum. So it is with adjusting to a disability. It's being much more aware of living on that spectrum. There will be good days and lousy days. During the lousy ones, you need to trust that better ones are coming.

REMEMBER:

- Keep a notebook for taking notes during doctor or lawyer visits
- Keep copies of everything your doctor or lawyer completes for you
- You are the manager of your healthcare; don't accept poor service
- Be honest with your family about your needs
- Consider having periodic family meetings in which you can discuss your situation, and everyone can talk about how they're feeling

Your thoughts:

_____

_____

_____

_____

_____

_____

_____

_____

_____

_____

Joy is a net of love
by which you can catch souls.

Mother Teresa

It isn't the moment you are struck
that you need courage, but for the long uphill
climb back to sanity, faith and security.
Lindbergh

Chapter 3

Silently Screaming

Okay, you've just been diagnosed with a new disability. Maybe it's Multiple Sclerosis (MS); perhaps it's the result of a car accident; maybe you've developed chronic fatigue syndrome; maybe you have a combat injury or a permanent work-related injury. Whatever the disability is, the result is the same. You're probably terrified and it's likely your family and friends are too.

We're not talking about "How much is the Visa bill?" kind of scared. We're talking about bone-chilling, mind-numbing terror. This fear is related to concerns about keeping your job, caring for your family, and maintaining your own bodily functions. And, what do you do about your hobbies? This fear can cut to the core of who you are. It can make you wonder if sticking around to see tomorrow is worth it. Your fears can be so big that they become too scary to share with your loved ones because you don't want to scare them.

Your family and friends are probably afraid of all of the same things you are. They're aching to take it from you. Whatever your particular disability is, they, like you, probably have had little or no exposure to disability. They're trying to be brave for you—just like you are for them. So, everyone holds it in and silently screams, hoping it passes.

Having this kind of fear is okay and "normal." It doesn't last forever. It just feels like it will. Good or bad, life forces us to get on with it. We can't stay frozen in the doctor's office or lie in the hospital forever. One day follows the next, and we have to go home and take care of life's details. We have to face the sunrise even when we're in shock.

More than likely, the fear will come in waves. Honor it when it comes. Don't belittle yourself or it. Let yourself feel an understandable reaction to having your world turned upside down.

A very wise woman once told me that fear is rarely constant. It rolls in and out like the waves on the lake. We're just unaccustomed to feeling something so strong that it seems constant. She said that if you allow fear and grief to roll in like the waves, they will certainly roll back out again. However, if we build a breakwater and try to stop the waves, they batter that wall mercilessly because the wall interferes with their natural path.

Our "breakwater" can be made of denial, physical tensing to ward it off (like clenching our jaw), burying ourselves in pills, alcohol, food, sleep, etc. We live in a society with a lot of control freaks. We often try to control every aspect of our lives. A disability teaches us that control is a pretty illusion that we have chosen to believe is real. We must release the need to control, especially now. It is the only way to survive these waves of fear. I urge you to stop building your wall or "breakwater." Your attempts at controlling your fear will only exhaust you. Let yourself feel the fear and know you'll move through it. It'll be back, but know you'll survive fear's future visits too.

During these times, be kind to yourself and find things (other than addictions) to comfort yourself. Talk to a friend or a professional; take a bath, or a long nap. Allow yourself some space and some quiet time. Allow yourself to cry. Allow yourself to feel what we former control freaks would've never allowed ourselves to feel before-- honest emotion based in the new and scary reality of the life we now have and never expected.

I've had trigeminal neuralgia for six years (it only seems like a lifetime), and I **still** have bouts of fear. I fear the bouts of pain. I fear trying to maintain my job through the next attack. I fear being a drag around my husband.

So let's deal with truth. Fear sucks! It's a rotten emotion to live with. Fear is the WORST foundation for decision making. **<u>Fear is not reality</u>**. It is our confused perception of things. It is not reality.

Never, never make big decisions from a place of fear. Let me say that again. Never, never make decisions out of fear. When a wave of fear has rolled in, it's hard to even decide if you should have tea or coffee because it's hard to think, period. So focus on breathing through it, trust it will pass, and NEVER allow yourself to make an important decision until you're calm and grounded.

Some types of big decisions that should not be made when fearful are:

-   If I can't control my bladder, how can I possibly keep my job? Maybe I should quit my job so I don't embarrass myself.

- Does this injury mean I can't have sex anymore? My spouse won't want me. Maybe I should file for a divorce.

- Does this embarrass my children? I won't go to their school activities anymore to spare them the embarrassment.

- Is there a way to live happily with this problem? Maybe I'll kill myself.

These thoughts may roll in with the waves of fear. Trust they'll roll back out and don't act on them. Instead, write them down and discuss them with your doctor. Find out how others have dealt with these same fears. Maybe there's a support group in your community for people with your same issue. If there isn't a local group, try to locate an on-line support group.

You might spare yourself a few bouts of fear by finding others with more experience and learning how they've coped. Seeing how others have survived might help you to accept that surviving is possible, that others have maintained jobs, families, sex lives, and have found that living is worth it. Once you know it's possible, the next wave of fear won't be quite as daunting.

I have always known that I was a lousy decision maker when I was afraid. I've always "bargained" with myself as a coping strategy. When I'm in fear and think things like "I can't handle this anymore. I should quit work" – I say in my head "You know you make lousy decisions when you're afraid. Let it go and pick it up again in a few months." This strategy has saved me from many poor choices that I would have regretted. I'm still working; I am still happily married; I'm still alive. None of these things would be true if I had made decisions based in fear.

REMEMBER:
- It's ok to be afraid
- Grief and loss are part of the healing process
- When fear or grief roll, in trust that they will certainly roll back out
- Never make decisions from a place of fear

Your thoughts:

_____

_____

_____

_____

_____

_____

_____

_____

_____

_____

_____

_____

_____

Life has to be taken
day by day, hour by hour.

C.S. Lewis

Chapter 4

Talk About "It"

Let's cut to the chase. No one wants to ever talk about any of the "its" in life because then "it" must be real. Denial is so much more appealing! Look at all the obvious "its" such as illness, hunger, poverty, death, etc. All these things are real and closer to us than we want to admit. It seems to me that we, as a society, just don't deal with reality very well. If we would discuss things boldly and bluntly, we'd all be so much healthier. Admitting that uncomfortable things are part of our existence might help us to feel less betrayed by God and by our bodies when "it" happens to us. (Thanks to T.C. for that pearl of wisdom.)

Talking about "it" also helps educate others and removes some of the stigma related to disability. It wasn't so long ago that issues such as domestic violence were taboo. Battered spouses had no resources, and society continued to turn a blind eye to their plight. Thankfully, a few brave souls started saying "No!" They refused to be shamed into maintaining the status quo.

Thanks to these people, we now have resources for survivors of domestic violence. Certainly there's room for improvement, but the issue isn't in the closet anymore.

We disabled adults need to keep this example in mind and keep our lives and our disabilities out of the closet. There is nothing to be ashamed of! Now, I'm not saying you should tattoo your disability on your forehead or shout it from the rooftops. I'm suggesting that we gently turn and face reality. Our reality with a disability is certainly different than it was before. Life is moving down a new and unfamiliar path. It's different, scary, and even lonely at times. All of that is real. All of that is part of the "it" that we don't want to talk about or admit could be our reality.

If we don't talk about "it" (our disability) we have a higher risk of falling into negative patterns like shame, blame, and excess. Shame will lead straight to depression. Blame or anger will make us, and those we love, miserable. Excesses such as alcoholism or over-eating have obvious painful consequences.

My suggestion is to gently face "it" or your new reality. Do this slowly and with kindness toward yourself. Acquiring a disability means you will undoubtedly have some grief and loss to deal with. Move gently down this road, but do move. Denying "it" or your pain won't make "it" go away. A skilled therapist can help you believe there really is life after disability.

Slowly discuss this with your family. Again, consider working with a therapist who specializes in grief and loss. Perhaps you could go to counseling together to address both your individual and shared fears or grief about "it." You might want to start using proper terminology to help in the reality check. Instead of saying "Mom/Dad is having a bad day," maybe start saying, "My amputation hurts" or "Dad's M.S. is flaring up" etc. Saying what it is can take the shame out of the big "it."

Of course, there are times when you may want to keep it simple or protect your privacy. As an example, if I'm planning to go to a restaurant for the first time, I usually call ahead to see if the facilities are accessible. I'm not going to launch into a discussion of my diagnosis because it's none of their business, and let's face it, that would just be weird. I simply say that I have a mobility impairment, and I need to know if the dining area and bathrooms are accessible.

Risks of talking too much –

As you adjust to your new disability and begin to feel your way through your new life, you may find yourself bouncing like a ball from one extreme to another. You may shut down and not realize it. For some of us, that's a coping strategy. Then you may realize, with some regret, that you just told your life story to your paperboy or to the cashier at the gas station. Don't worry about it. Swinging between the extremes is normal until you find your own center. Again, a good therapist can help with this.

So why talk about the big "it"? Your new disability does not need to become the main topic at dinner three times per week. I'm only suggesting you start to talk about "it" so you can reach a point of personal comfort with your new reality. Further, by admitting your new reality, you'll be more likely to admit your needs.

I've worked with many people who had a permanent injury that was painful every day. Either they hadn't explained it well to their family, or the family members weren't tuned in. The result is often that, when the person asked for help, they were ignored. Asking for help in itself is painful. Being ignored is devastating, so they would just do whatever needed to be done by themselves. This exacerbates pain, frustration, and exhaustion.

During the years that I've worked with people with disabilities, this same theme has presented itself over and over in family after family. What I learned is that people can't ask for help until they admit there's a problem. Family and friends need to understand that there is a problem in order to understand why their help is needed. That's why the first step is to face that big "it".

Now that we've established that talking about your disability is important, lets talk about the "extremes" that are better to be avoided.

To all of you well-intentioned loved ones: **DO NOT USE THIS BOOK TO FORCE ANYONE TO DO ANYTHING THEY'RE NOT READY TO DO!**

After writing about the need to face up to the big "it" of disability, I had a wave of fear wash over me. I could just picture a well-meaning spouse, parent, or friend using my suggestions to verbally beat their loved into talking "because the book says you have to." Au contraire! This book does not say that the person with the disability has to or **should** do anything. I am merely suggesting a path toward healing. Trust that your newly disabled loved one needs to do what's right for them in their own time. Don't force them to talk if they're not ready. Allow them to grieve and to heal at their own pace.

Another "extreme" in behavior that I personally think is counter productive is excessive joking about your disability. Sometimes people with disabilities feel that making jokes about their situation puts others at ease. I did this when I was younger, and then had to deal with the fall-out. A low key quip may be acceptable on occasion. However, joking too much can backfire. It can be offensive to more conservative people. It can also give the impression that others can feel free to joke about it too. You may find that when someone else jokes about you or your situation it feels hurtful or insulting. This can be a tough situation to turn around or rein in because you started it. Just be cautious with jokes.

One more "extreme" is to watch that your talking doesn't turn into constant complaining. Usually, your loved ones will do their best to understand and support you. However, they can't feel your pain or take it away. They need to understand your condition, what helps and what hurts. Just be careful not to have every conversation be about you. It will get old for them. If you really need to vent, my suggestion is to see a qualified therapist. You can go in and purge all your emotional stuff, and they can help you through it.

I simply can't stress enough the benefits a good therapist can provide. Or again—check out your closest support group.

REMEMBER:

- Facing the big "it" helps all involved
- Talk about what you need, what helps and what hurts
- Let your family in on your new reality
- Consider individual and family counseling
- Avoid joking too much about your disability
- Keep loved ones informed but avoid complaining

Your thoughts:

_____

_____

_____

_____

_____

_____

_____

_____

_____

_____

_____

_____

_____

To a friend's house, the road
is never long.

Anonymous

Nothing in life is to be feared, it is only to be understood. Now is the time to understand more, so that we can fear less.

Marie Curie

Chapter 5

What If ......

When you deal with loss, there are so many fears that go through your head. We touched on this before. Making decisions based on fear is a bad move. But what do you do with the fear?

Here's a little game I play. I take whatever fear is eating at me, and I play it out in my mind in the worst-case scenario. I call this my "What if" game. So let's try one. How about a common fear such as: "Can I go back to work? What if I can't do my job with my new disability/challenge?" This is a common fear.

If it were me, I'd roll that around in my head, and I'd address the critical survival issues first.

So, if I couldn't do my job with my disability, I'd apply for whatever funding I may be entitled to. Is it a Worker's Compensation injury? Then I'd start developing close communication with my Worker's Comp insurance carrier. It's a good idea to educate yourself on your state's worker's comp laws and your rights for income while you're in the healing process. Find out who is handling your case at the Worker's Comp. insurance firm. Get their full name, their supervisor's name, and direct phone numbers for both parties. Keep a notebook next to the phone. Write down what they tell you to do and whatever else they say so that you can follow through with their requirements.

I'd apply for all available services to survive. This would include Social Security disability benefits, welfare programs through the state, fuel assistance, food stamps, etc. I would find out about food pantries in the area. Now, some will see this as defeat. I see it as employing effective coping and survival skills during a crisis situation. This is precisely what these programs are for; you don't need to use them forever.

Once you've addressed the survival issues, then start considering the next level. Perhaps you could consult with your employer about modifying your job so you could do it. An occupational therapist could be brought in to discuss modifications. If your old job can't be modified, ask them if there is something else you could do for them within your restrictions.

Now let's go to the next level. What if you just can't go back to your job? Maybe there's a different option. Maybe you can go back to school and get trained for something else. This may be the back-up plan that gives you peace of mind. Consult with your State's Vocational Rehabilitation Division for assistance. Worker's Comp may also contribute to your retraining if your disability is work related.

Did you see what we did? We took an anxiety-provoking fear and played it out until we had a back-up plan. When you have another plan you won't be so fearful.

I do mini-versions of this every day. I try to plan ahead too. For example, thanks to my medication, I fall more often. Getting up by myself is difficult. Sometimes it's impossible. When it started happening more often, I was afraid of it occurring at work. Well, it does happen at work. I'm obviously embarrassed, but I live with it. Someone is always kind enough to help me up. I shake off the embarrassment and go on. However, I know getting up by myself at work is not something I want to deal with. The furniture in the office isn't sturdy enough. I've played the scenario out. I know it's not safe. I'm careful to never be alone at work.

Planning ahead and playing out the scenarios can help relieve anxiety. So, the next time you have a fear tugging at your sanity, take that worst-case scenario, problem solve your way through it in your head, and see if you don't feel better! Once you stare down the worst, the rest isn't as bad.

I believe that fear takes many forms. It might manifest as anger, moodiness, depression, etc. Many of these conditions are rooted in fear. Deal with the fear, and these other issues will improve too.

Try this – the next time you're feeling a negative emotion, honestly ask yourself "What am I afraid of?" First, you'll probably think "Dinah's an idiot. I'm mad, not afraid." Then you may spend some time rationalizing. That's okay. Keep working at it and keep being honest. Peel away each layer. See if you find a seed or two of fear deep down. Maybe being mad helps you work through the fear of what others are thinking or whatever is bothering you. By dealing with the fear, you'll release the anger more easily. If you don't deal with the fear it'll just keep popping up with other names.

A friend of mine is a huge fan of the " *Course in Miracles* " and has studied it for years. "The Course" states that there are only two core emotions, love and fear. You're either in one or the other. I believe this is true and worthy of your attention as you heal. When you can pinpoint what you're afraid of, you can problem solve through it.

Let's say you're afraid of falling when you're alone. Consider putting a phone in each room so you can easily call for help if you need to. You could also check into an emergency alert system which enables you to just press a button (on a necklace that you always wear), that calls someone to check on you. Would this calm your fear and help you be at peace?

What if you can't control what you're afraid of? Lets say your fear is based in not being accepted as you are now? What if you drift away from family and friends? Well you can't control them. You can only control you and your thoughts. In this case, the problem solving would need to come through working to be more comfortable with who you are now. The more at peace you are with your disability, the less other people's opinions will matter.

Another helpful tool for dealing with fear is the use of affirmations. An affirmation is a positive statement that you repeat many times each day for as least six to eight weeks. Affirmations can, when used properly, assist in improving self-esteem, weight loss, and overall health.

Let's say you choose to use affirmations to improve your acceptance of who you are now. By feeling okay about who you are, by choosing to love yourself as you are, you choose well-being over fear and pain.

Take time to construct a simple statement that addresses your specific chosen issue. An example might be:

"I am beautiful, strong and at peace with myself. I trust that divine love flows through me constantly and helps me continue to heal in mind, body, and spirit."

Try this or something that feels better to you. Say your

affirmation as often as you can throughout the day. Use it for about six to eight weeks. What you're doing by repeating this many times throughout the day is creating new thought patterns. Your inner critic, that voice in your head that corrects you, points out your flaws, and reminds you of embarrassing situations, is well developed after years of criticizing you. Using affirmations is a way of counteracting the inner critic. You are using these positive statements to develop a new habit, a new way of looking at yourself. You are reprogramming your brain, if you will.

One thing to remember when developing your affirmation is to say everything in the present tense, such as: "I accept myself. I love myself." By saying that as though it already is, you are reprogramming your brain to believe that it **is true** now. If, for example, you would say "I will accept myself" you are postponing it and always putting it just out of reach.

If affirmations feel right to you, consider reading Louise Hay's book, *You can Heal Your Life*. You might also want to consider the suggested reading list at the end of this book.

Having fear in your life, especially now, is normal. It doesn't have to consume you. You can decide between fear and love and then, hopefully, pursue love.

REMEMBER:

- Play the "What if" game. Work through the worst case scenario of your fear until you come up with a possible plan
- Be aware of your emotions and see if deep down you find a seed of fear at the base of every negative emotion
- Address fear through affirmations
- Affirmations can help retrain that inner critic

Your thoughts:

_____

_____

_____

_____

_____

_____

_____

_____

_____

_____

_____

Only when the winds of adversity show
can you tell whether an individual or
a country has courage and steadfastness.

John F. Kennedy

Prayer begins where human capacity ends.

Marion Anderson

Chapter 6

Feeding Your Spirit

Recovery from any kind of grief or loss can occur more easily when you feed your spirit. Healing happens more thoroughly when you ignite the "mind-body-spirit" connection. Think for a moment about Olympic athletes. They train hard. But they don't just work their muscles. They maintain good nutrition, get enough sleep, and drink enough water. Many of them use affirmations and visualization. They envision themselves winning because it's important that they believe it's possible. Many also use some kind of spirituality, prayer, or meditation to help them stay grounded.

If you don't have some kind of spirituality in your life, think about what might appeal to you. I'm not talking about church; however, if that's your chosen form of spiritual expression, go for it! Spirituality is a belief in something bigger than yourself. Spirituality in its purest form can bring you joy. It touches your heart. Spirituality can help you feel connected to others and helps you get clearer about yourself.

Some people get this kind of uplifting experience in nature. Some get it from poetry, music, or painting. Take a moment and think about what experiences have brought you joy. Was it sharing time with friends? Have you been joyful reading a good book or watching a good movie? What touches your heart? Whatever brings you pure joy is something to consider pursuing. Joy will help in the healing process.

Everyone knows you have to eat and drink in order to keep your body alive and functioning. Without proper nutrition, the body withers.

The same is true for your spirit, the part of you that is more than your body, more than your mind, the part of you that is everlasting; that part of you needs the kind of nourishment that only faith can provide. There is no "right" way toward feeding your spirit. You'll know when you've found your own spiritual food because it will provide you with a sense of peace, comfort, and well being. That sense of peace or comfort may come from the Bible or maybe from the Scriptures of other faiths. Maybe you'll experience this peace through a sunset or through your own prayer and meditation. Whatever brings you this type of inner calm is worth repeating regularly

I'm not saying that pursuing spirituality will solve your problems. Whether you're the person with the new disability or the person who loves him/her, you have a long road ahead of you. Spirituality doesn't change the road. Spirituality is more like the shock absorbing system on your vehicle. It will help you handle the bumps in your road more gracefully. Feeding your spirit will help you to remember that you **can** survive the bumps, and that the road will get smoother again if you just hang on and ride it out.

Know too that your spirituality will grow and change as you do. For a while, maybe the sunset will be enough to bring you peace. Often, when we're in crisis (as we are with the onset of a new disability), we simply can't handle a lot of input or stimulation. We have all we can do to get through the day. It's not typically a time when we can digest deeper concepts.

In the early days after the onset of a disability, the beauty of a sunset or deer grazing in a field is enough. Surviving each day and recognizing beauty before us is sometimes all we can handle. Don't be surprised though, when the time comes when your spirit demands more. This is likely to be cyclical.

As you adjust to your disability and some of the crisis feeling melts away, you'll likely have the ability to digest more. You might find yourself wanting the sunset AND other inspirations as well. Honor this feeling and feed your spirit. Maybe you'll want to explore other thoughts or traditions. Perhaps you'll want to go to a church, synagogue, or some other place of worship to share time and space with a faith community. Maybe there's a Native American community near you that is open to non-traditionals sharing some of their ceremonies. Only you know what's right for you. Follow your heart.

Maybe you'll go down a few dead ends in your search and that's all right. Exploration, even if some of the paths taken end up to be not right for you, will help you to reach what **is** right for you. It'll also help you to more easily recognize the paths that aren't right for you in future searches.

For me, the need to feed my Spirit has taken me from middle-of-the-road religion to a short stint in a very strict religion, to studying with a Native American medicine woman, to participating in a women's spirituality circle, to now being more of a lone meditation and prayer person. What I learned through all of that is that we are supported, whether we choose to know it or not. God or Spirit or a Higher Power or whatever you want to call Him/Her/It is there for us. We aren't on our own. We have heaven and all its inhabitants cheering us on. This knowing, this belief in more and what it means for our lives, is precisely what our spirits need as we heal.

I've gone through periods where I've been downright mad at God and the angels that are supposed to help me. In my head I've thought "How can God allow this?" I guess I thought I was immune or something because I already had one disability. Well, I'm not immune, but I am supported. When the pain gets especially bad, I can get angry again. I had always heard that God would never give you more than you can handle. If that's true, then God thinks I can handle more than I think I'm capable of. But let's face it; there is nothing easy about a disability, especially if it involves chronic pain.

So, while it's true that God and I have not always been on speaking terms, we've always had a relationship. That's the cycle I referred to before. When I'm in severe pain, my relationship with God or Spirit may only go as deep as appreciating the sunset because that's all I'm capable of. When the pain lessens, my relationship goes deeper through my own meditation and prayer. I don't criticize or judge myself when I'm less connected. I think God knows that I'm doing the best I can. I think that's all we can ask of ourselves or others. Trust yourself. Don't judge the cycles that may come where you are more or less involved in spirituality. But do feed your spirit in whatever manner you can. Your healing journey can only be improved by feeding your spirit.

REMEMBER:
- Ignite your mind-body-spirit connection
- Feeding your spirit will help you heal
- What your spirit needs is likely to be cyclical. Trust that.
- Follow what brings you joy

Your thoughts:

_____

_____

_____

_____

_____

_____

_____

_____

_____

_____

_____

_____

_____

I set my star so high that I
would constantly be in motion towards it.

Sidney Poitier

Chapter 7

Nutrition and Movement

Food may or may not have been something you gave much attention to prior to your disability. For me, food has always been a necessary inconvenience. I used to skip breakfast, eat whatever I could find in my desk for lunch (usually a granola bar) and then eat a semi-decent dinner. When hunger hit during the day I'd shove a cookie or a spoonful of peanut butter in my mouth and I'd keep going. This was before the trigeminal neuralgia hit.

Food has just never been a big deal for me. It still isn't. However, it is something I'm forced to pay attention to now. Because of my medication, I have to eat and eat <u>smart</u>. My skipping breakfast days are gone. I need protein three times each day. I don't need to stuff myself but I do need to eat. If I don't eat I get even more tired and light-headed from the medication. I know my productivity decreases because my medication hits me harder without food to soften the blow.

Did my doctor or pharmacist clue me in on the need for food with my medication? Of course not! Initially I'd take my morning dose, go to work, feel like I just couldn't think, and hope it would pass as I adjusted to the medication. I started to realize eating helped. As I monitored what I ate and how I felt, I realized I felt better if I ate an egg or other protein than if I just had cereal or toast. Let's face it, much of this journey is trial and error.

I am by no means an expert on nutrition. I know what works for me and I believe in using common sense with food. For instance, you need to realize that your body has been compromised by your disability. You may lack the strength and resiliency you once had. Look at your 'pre-disability' habits. Did you tend to skip meals and it was no big deal? Well it may be a big deal now. You may feel the consequences quickly in the form of weakness, shakiness, fatigue, confusion, or increased pain. The days of abusing your body by not feeding it are behind you. It's time to take good care of what you have.

It is also important to see yourself as a whole being with all systems being interrelated. If you fail to feed your body, all your other systems will be impacted. You won't think as clearly or be as strong or cope as well.

Now, what if you have had the opposite tendencies? What do you do about overeating? My suggestion is to see a qualified dietician or nutritionist and to seriously cultivate some healthier habits. Often, when someone acquires a new disability, their activity level decreases. It's important that your food intake matches your activity level because weight will be a problem if you don't watch this.

If you have a problem with binge eating, my suggestion is to keep a good supply of fresh fruit and vegetables in the house and get rid of the chips and junk food. If you need to nibble away some nervous energy, you won't do damage by diving into the apple or celery stash.

My feeling is that skipping meals or eating a lot of junk or stuffing yourself repeatedly are all luxuries that people with disabilities can't indulge in if they want to maintain strength and quality of life. Food is fuel that needs to be chosen and used wisely.

I recently started following the glycemic index weight management program. The program that I use is based upon the work of Dr. Sheri Liebermann and it's called the Transitions program. You can find out more about this program through her book DARE TO LOSE and/or The G.I. DIET books by Gallop.

This is a simple way of eating that keeps your blood sugar stable so that you burn more of what you eat and reduce your overall body fat. It's also a much healthier approach to weight management. The emphasis is on vegetables and lean protein. It's a sensible way of eating for life.

In a perfect world, I'd be able to eat as many chocolate chip cookies as I want and still look great! Unfortunately, that isn't the case. My cookies started showing more after the BIG 4-0 birthday hit me so I realized I needed to do something. The Transitions program made sense to me and it has helped me manage my weight. This is crucial for me as a disabled adult. The heavier I get, the harder it is to walk.

As for movement and exercise......DO IT! How simple, right? Hardly!! Non-disabled people have a hard time dragging their butts off the couch. It's often even harder for people with disabilities because they often feel rotten as it is. It's hard to justify using limited energy on exercise. I could list ten reasons or <u>excuses</u> to get out of exercising without batting an eye, and they would all be true. They don't matter though.

The only thing that matters is that you do what you can do to preserve what you have. If your disability is physical, I would suggest talking to your doctor and getting him/her to approve an exercise routine from a physical therapist so you know that all of the movements involved are good for you and safe.

I work with a friend/physical therapy assistant/personal trainer—yes, Mikealynn is all of these things. She is also a genius when it comes to developing exercise programs for people. I recently told her about a new realization I had. I exercise at home as well as at the physical therapy gym. Most of my exercises are simply moving my body, such as lying on my back and doing leg lifts or lying on my side and again lifting my leg. I realized that one of the reasons I hate working out is that it depresses me. It frustrates the hell out of me to struggle to simply lift my leg.

I told Mikealynn that it feels better to work on machinery because then I'm pushing against something other than my own body weight. Struggling on a weight machine is somehow less depressing to me than struggling against my own body.

Mikealynn told me that this is a very common feeling and also that it is quite upside-down. Moving your own body weight through space is much more beneficial than working against a machine. Most people prefer weight training but the overall benefits are more limited. She went into discussing some very technical studies that have been done, measuring the firing of the nerves and muscles together during weight or machine exercise as well as during exercise that only involved moving the body (such as leg lifts, push-ups, etc).

I can't discuss it as well as she does, but I can tell you that the bottom line of the studies was that the nerves and muscles derived more benefit from simply moving the body than from working on machinery. If you stop to think about it, you have to see that this makes sense. Weight or resistance training tends to isolate the groups of muscles that are being worked. Moving a particular body part forces you to recruit more muscle groups because it's an overall motion, not an isolated one.

As an example, when I do the dreaded leg lift, I feel the muscles tightening in my stomach, my hip, my butt, my leg and even in the leg I'm not lifting because that leg is stabilizing my body weight. A machine would not force me to employ all of those muscle groups. Moving my body weight forces me to become more balanced in all the muscle groups.

This isn't new science. Look at Tai Chi or Pilates. It's the same principle. Strengthen the body as a unit, not as isolated parts because the body **is** a whole unit, not just a bunch of random puzzle pieces.

So, the good news is that this recent conversation just saved me $1500 because the idea of buying a home gym flew out the window. The bad news is that now I'm a little smarter, I know a little more about the need to exercise and the benefits. So, if I don't do it I'm being even more irresponsible in caring for my body. Knowledge can be a burden.

However, knowledge is also power. The more I know about caring for my body, the better I'll feel. I've gotten more serious about exercise and I am feeling better. Am I running marathons? No. But at work I'm not wondering if my legs will get me to the bathroom either. My legs feel sturdier.

So, talk to someone who can educate you about caring for your body, disability and all. You won't ever regret caring properly for the one and only body you have!!

If your disability is not physical, I'd still suggest asking a professional to help you develop an exercise program so that you get maximum benefit from what you do. I believe that studies have shown that exercise also improves your mood because it releases endorphins. Endorphins help to elevate your general outlook.

Of course, once you have an exercise routine, then you have to actually do it. This is a constant challenge for me. I exercise with a friend and that has helped a lot. You may want to try this or a personal reward system. Do whatever you need to do to exercise – DO IT. It will preserve your strength and will help to improve your outlook on life.

Remember:
- Knowledge is power
- Use food as fuel and fuel your body as you would your car
- Learn what you need to do to preserve what you have
- You don't need fancy equipment. You just need a qualified professional to show you what movements will be safe and beneficial for you.
- Your body is an interrelated system. Neglecting one part will impact everything else.

Your thoughts:

_____

_____

_____

_____

_____

_____

_____

_____

_____

In friendship we walk more miles
together than even the poets dreamed possible.

Unknown

Don't worry about oppositions.
Remember, a kite rises against the wind
not with the wind.

Hamilton Wright Mabie

Chapter 8

Loneliness

Loneliness – it's a tough pill to swallow. For some, it's positively shocking. Prior to the onset of their disability, many people were loners. They were self-sufficient and not incredibly social. So, if they didn't need people before, why are they lonely now? Everyone's situation is different, but here's my guess. Before their disability arrived on the scene, many of these folks were busy. Their time was probably filled with work and running through life. After their disability, life slowed down and now there are some empty hours that can feel very long. This is especially true if they can't return to work. Work, for as much of a drag as it can be, provides structure to our day as well as a type of automatic socialization. Without that, even "loners" can feel lonely.

And, how about the social butterflies? Prior to their disability, they had lots of friends. How could they be lonely? First of all, the same is true for these people. If they're not going back to their jobs, there's a big hole in their day.

After acquiring a disability, some may find that they just aren't hearing from many of the people they thought were friends. How can this be? How could friends not stay in touch? A common reaction to this is to blame yourself because you choose to interpret their actions as confirmation that you are now less than you were before. I would highly doubt that this is accurate.

Consider this: Many of us are clueless when it comes to handling our own grief, much less supporting someone else through theirs. Few of us ever learned how to confront raw emotion in a gentle, supportive way. Most of us are taught to "ignore it or forget about it" and keep going through the motions of everyday life until the big "it" passes, whatever "it" is.

I suggest you, as the person with the disability, help people through this if you feel up to the challenge. If you find your friends act awkwardly around you, gently confront them. You can say "I know this is weird. Is there anything you want to know or ask me?" Maybe they want to know if you're in pain or if the doctors feel you'll improve. The dynamics with your friends will likely change over time. Encounters will be less awkward as you both adjust.

When in doubt, ask! We're all taught that it's not polite to pry, so we all live thinking we know the answers to our unanswered questions when we may not. Think of how kids ask about everything so easily. They want to understand something so they ask; it's that simple. We can learn a lot from kids.

--A side bar—So many times throughout my life little kids see me walking with crutches and spontaneously say something like, "Mom, what's wrong with her? Or Why does she walk like that?" Many times the horrified parent grabs the kids and moves away quickly, saying something like "Shhh, that's not polite!" If possible, before they flee, I try to gently smile at the child and simply say "Hi Sweetie, I use crutches because I'm not very strong and they help me walk better." It's important to me that kids be able to see that disabilities are not things to never be spoken of; they're just another "normal" part of life!

There may be some friends who completely fall by the wayside. Don't take this personally. It doesn't mean you're not worthy. It more likely means that they simply don't have the coping skills to confront discomfort or grief. It might also remind them of their own human frailty or vulnerability and that just scares the hell out of them. Don't take on their stuff. It's theirs to deal with. Release them with loving thoughts, knowing they're doing the best they can. Harboring resentment toward them only hurts you.

Appreciate friends and family who do remain in touch. Remember to be gracious, and to thank them for their love and support. You don't have to always wait for them to call you. Friendship and phone lines go both ways. It's not fair to put all the responsibility on them. They don't know what you can and can't handle, so maybe you have to be the one to suggest going out to lunch or to a movie. That will help them to know what feels "do-able" for you. They may not have suggested it for fear of tiring you or hurting you. Reach out to your family and friends.

Reaching out is especially difficult for men. Most men don't talk about feelings or problems with each other. They talk about work, sports, hunting, news, etc. They rarely discuss personal issues. Because most men don't discuss these things easily, their emotions and frustrations often become bottled up inside them.

Men often feel like a volcano ready to erupt at any minute. Many people who have trouble expressing themselves or find it hard to reach out to friends will just hold it all in until they yell at their spouse because the coffee is cold (and their yelling has nothing to do with the coffee). They might cry privately or find some other way to release the pent up frustration. If their disability prevents them from engaging in their former hobbies, they may start to feel that they have nothing to talk about. They often withdraw from most everyone because they're worried they will either complain or explode.

For those of you who fall into this category, I would encourage you to find a good counselor to help you deal with your frustration. You don't have to live like a human volcano.

I would also encourage you to reach out to your old friends. Maybe you can't throw a bowling ball anymore. That doesn't mean you can't go and hang out with them while they bowl. Sure it might feel weird at first, but so what. They're your friends. Allow them to get to know this "you" that is different but is still you. Reach out.

If you find that you still have too much empty time, consider hobbies you can develop. Try reading. If reading is difficult, try books on tape. Can you take an art class? Consider support groups where you can interact with others who have similar challenges.

For you family and friends who may read this as a way of understanding your newly disabled loved one, take a deep breath. You want to support them and yet you may not know how. My suggestion is to ask them if there's anything they need help doing. There might be things around the house that need to be done that they can't do. Asking for help is hard to do, especially in the beginning. Offering to help is a way to lighten their burden both emotionally and physically.

If they don't need help, then just be with them. You can listen if they feel like talking. You can fill them in on what's new with you. Just hang out. Your company is a gift in and of itself.

A disability isn't something to be fixed. It's a new way of life for everyone to adjust to. Just take it slowly. There may be some awkward moments. That's okay. Take it slowly and trust that you'll all find your way.

When I was diagnosed with trigeminal neuralgia and had the big ER visit/med problem, and then was unable to walk alone for almost a month, I was very fortunate. During that time, I had friends who would come by and just hang out with me. This gave my husband a break. He felt better about leaving the house knowing I wasn't alone. There was no agenda with these friends, no right or wrong. We just hung out.

As I said before, just the presence of a friend is enough. Initially, you may both be uncomfortable. Trust in your heart that your presence can ease their burden. Isn't this what you'd want and need if the situation were reversed?

REMEMBER:

- Reach out to your family and friends
- Ask for help
- Friendship and phone lines go both ways
- Reach out

Your thoughts:

_____

_____

_____

_____

_____

_____

_____

_____

_____

_____

_____

_____

_____

*If you would be loved,
love and be loveable.*

Ben Franklin

Heaven is under our feet
as well as over our heads.
Thoreau

Chapter 9

Resistance

We talked before about not resisting or tensing against emotions as they come. There's another level of resistance we need to talk about. Before we do that though, let me explain the picture above.

Near my former home, there was a beautiful old tree that the city, in its infinite wisdom, cut down. After they hauled away the pieces, I drove past the spot feeling sad that the tree was gone. What I noticed though, was pretty amazing. The tree had been growing near a power pole and lines. There was about a two foot chunk of the tree still hanging on one of the wires. They had never removed it. The tree, as it grew, had grown around the wire!!

When I saw that, I was stunned by the beauty of this as a metaphor for our lives. Think about it. That tree was there long before the power pole and lines were installed. Someone decided the lines had to be placed there, so it was done. The tree kept growing and eventually grew up against the wire.

Now I'm sure it was uncomfortable at first. The wire surely had to be pressing into that branch more and more as the tree grew. But think about what that tree did. It didn't give up and die. It didn't lose that branch from discomfort. Those would have been acts of resistance. Had the tree resisted, the end result would have harmed the tree itself. Nature is too smart for that.

Instead, the tree grew **around and with** the wire! The tree actually incorporated the wire into itself and kept growing. That is the ultimate act of nonresistance – consider the beauty in that simple action of acceptance. The tree couldn't change the wire, so it invited the wire in and they became one. Nature is brilliant!

What can we learn from this?

We can push against our new condition. We can hate it and/or deny it. We can engage in any number of negative self-defeating actions or emotions. We can even give up. But what if we chose to accept it rather than resist it? What if we incorporated it as part of who we are now instead of resisting it? What if we chose to keep growing with this new condition as a part of who we are, like the tree that grew with the wire as part of itself?

Try to consider these questions as possibilities in your life. If you can entertain these suggestions, then you can choose growth as a possibility. You can allow your disability to be your catalyst rather than your stumbling block. Let it spark new growth for you rather than being what breaks you! That's what the tree did. Would it be possible to trust that there is Universal

Wisdom or Divine Guidance at work even in this difficult time?

Now, is all this easier said then done? Absolutely! Did you like change and inconvenience before your disability? Most of us don't enjoy change and having to work harder at things. But let's face it, not liking something never changes it. Fighting against things just depletes you. You don't have to like it. However, the more you actively resist your disability by complaining or just giving up, the harder it is on you.

If I would ever be magically granted three wishes, you can be sure I'd ditch both of my disabilities in a heartbeat! I hate chronic pain! And frankly, walking with crutches my whole life hasn't been anywhere near my idea of fun. That said, can I see Divine Wisdom at work? YES! "How?" you ask. Well, I'm human and I have a lot of rather obvious personality flaws. I think my disabilities have sanded down some of the sharper edges of my personality. I think it also added compassion to my outlook on life.

So, I give myself permission not to be thrilled with being disabled. However, I won't use it as a reason to give up on life. Again, resisting your disability doesn't change anything. A friend taught me an expression: "That which we resist, persists!" -- In other words, the more you push against something in a negative manner, the more it stays the same.

When we can't change an external situation our only alternative is to change our mind or our outlook.

So, back to where we were before. Can you use your disability to propel yourself into a better place or to become a better person? Whenever you're in doubt, back up and remember that tree and wire story. Consider inviting your disability to be part of your life, and then keep growing! You can do it. **Nature doesn't lie.**

REMEMBER:
- Resistance depletes you
- Acceptance can be empowering
- You have choices
- You have the ability to embrace these challenges and keep growing
- Trust that there is Divine Wisdom and Guidance available to you

Your thoughts:

_____

_____

_____

_____

_____

_____

_____

_____

_____

_____

_____

Angels can fly because
they take themselves lightly.

G.K. Chesterton

Each day comes bearing its own
gifts. Untie the ribbons.

Ruth Ann Schubacker

Chapter 10

Dealing with Failure

Ahh, the 'F' word. It's so nasty! Do we really even want it in our vocabulary? Probably not but it's there isn't it? So let's deal with it.

When you can't do what you did before, that judgmental voice that we talked about earlier pops up with some ugly words. It'll also crop up if you have to do things differently than before.

Time for another story to make my point:

As you know, I grew up with my mobility impairment. I therefore grew up "chasing normal." I walked with crutches even then, but I was determined not to use anything else –no braces, no scooter and no wheelchair. In my mind, crutches were failure enough. They made me look different, and I wanted to look "normal."

I went to college for a year and a half in a beautiful old city in the South. Many of my friends would go to shops, bars, and restaurants in the old downtown district. I could never go along because they walked there. Cars weren't allowed. The main street was only for pedestrians.

My dad offered to buy a scooter for me so that I could go there too. I was mortified at the very idea. In my mind, that would make me look far more disabled – and keep me farther from "normal." I believed that I didn't need to go anywhere that I couldn't walk to myself. Consequently, I never saw the most beautiful part of the city.

Fast forward twenty years to the person I am today. I still try to walk as much as possible, but I use a scooter for distance. Two years, ago my husband and I went back to that old college town. I hadn't been there in 20 years, and I wanted him to see it. I had my scooter, and I finally got to see the downtown area. It was lovely and so quaint!

It saddened me to realize that I had cheated myself out of seeing it and being a part of it when I was younger. My fear of failure and my need to "chase normal" significantly diminished my ability to experience and enjoy the world around me.

Would using a scooter in college really have meant failure? I'm older now and just a little bit wiser. Now I know that choosing to avoid something that could assist me only hurts me. I had a visible disability whether I chose to use the scooter or not. Not using a scooter didn't make me look less disabled.

Now let me clarify something. I'm not promoting dependence on technology if you don't need it. I will defend my right to choose to walk for as long as possible. When I go to the grocery store, I walk and push a cart instead of using a scooter. It has nothing to do with how I look. It's because I want the exercise. Again, that's my right and my choice to make.

I'm suggesting looking at the reasoning **behind** your decisions.

If you're choosing not to use an assistive device because you're trying to maintain your strength, that's great! If, however, you choose not to use an assistive device because you're afraid of how you'll look or what people will think of you, then I would suggest that you re-think your decision. None of us can or should do anything that doesn't feel right. I'm not suggesting that. Ask yourself why you're making your decision not to use assistive devices or counseling or medical treatment or whatever your personal need is. Could it be because of the "F" word –failure?

We might want to ask ourselves if using a brace, a scooter, a hearing aid, or going to a counselor would add to or detract from our current lifestyle. If it will enhance communication, independence, or self-esteem, go for it! If, however, you're just not ready, or if taking that step is too frightening or painful, then wait. You'll know when you're ready. Let's face the facts. Using assistive devices can feel like further confirmation that the big "it," your disability, is real. Give yourself time to adjust and be gentle with yourself.

Another example of this in my own life is in my recent decision to try leg/ankle braces (A.F.O.'s) for the third time. My doctor recommended them ten years ago. At that time, I got some "off the shelf," meaning they weren't personally fitted. I wore them twice, hated them, and tossed them in the closet. They are meant to keep people with weak ankles from catching their toe on the floor when they don't lift their foot high enough, thus preventing falls.

I hated the way they felt, and I worried that using them would make my ankles weaker. So I decided it was better to do without them. And, truthfully, I didn't like the thought of the way AFO's would look. Three years ago, my knees started buckling more. I saw an orthotist, (someone who can custom make braces or "orthotics") and this time they custom made a brace for my left ankle. I hated this second one even more! It was too bulky and rigid. When I told the orthotist who made it that it felt bulky and awkward, he told me to get used to it. I never wore it even once. It was uncomfortable.

Recently, I met with a new orthotist. He actually listened to me and tried to understand what bothered me about the other braces. He created something lighter and less rigid. He also encouraged me to work in partnership with him by telling him if something felt wrong or uncomfortable because, even though the braces were tailor made for me, they would need minor adjustments before they'd feel good.

We discussed my fear about my ankles getting weaker. The orthotist and the physical therapist suggested that I not wear them at home so that my ankles wouldn't get too much weaker. At one point the physical therapist, who knows me well, said "Dinah, these won't be pretty." I assured her that, at 41, I wasn't concerned about pretty anymore. I was concerned about falling less. She then said, "Yeah, falling on the floor is none too pretty either I guess!" We laughed at that but it's true. I'm now at a point where I'm falling more often from not picking my foot up high enough. Now that I've dealt with some painful falls, the appearance of braces takes a back seat to being able to walk safely.

It took me ten years to get to this point. To some that may sound strange. But it was the right time frame for me. I now feel that the "trade-off" of braces versus falling is worth it. I wasn't falling enough before to feel that it was a worthwhile trade-off. I also have to admit that, even though it feels like the right decision, it still feels a bit like failure. I feel like I messed up in some way by not staying strong enough to walk without braces. That's the judgmental inner-critic that loves to spread blame and shame. I'm making a concerted effort to think differently. Feeling like I failed is just victimizing myself and that depletes my energy. Frankly, that's not how I want to use my energy. Instead, when that negativity creeps into my head, I list all of the reasons that it's not true. This forces me to look at my successes –how refreshing!

Could it be that our inner critic is just a big, fat liar that we need to ignore at all costs? What if we retrained our inner voice to be a gentle supporter of who we are and who we are becoming? What if we recreated the critic into a coach that reminded us of the good we've done and kept encouraging us to do more good tomorrow? Life is all about choices. Isn't it exciting to think that we actually have a choice about how we view ourselves and how we talk to ourselves? We really can decide to change the messages we give ourselves all day long. We can create a supportive inner voice.

Think about this for a moment. For most people, the "default" message, the one that comes to mind automatically, is critical of us. This may have started in childhood when peer pressure is high and the need to be like everyone else is paramount. Perhaps it's due to all of the media foolishness that makes people think they've failed if they don't look like one of the ten super models. The great part about internal messages though is that we can change them!

You can review the section on affirmations (found in the "What If..." chapter) as one great way to change your thoughts. A recurring thought is like a well traveled path in the woods. It has been walked on so many times that it is the easiest one to take. That's why your brain pulls it up so often. We have criticized ourselves so many times that, when we get into an uncomfortable situation, our brain pops up the critical thought because it presumes that's what we're looking for.

Suppose you're in the grocery store and you reach for a jar of mayonnaise and you drop it. Maybe it's disability related, maybe not. You're suddenly in an embarrassing situation. Your brain then offers you a list of thoughts you've used in other embarrassing situations such as: "Stupid! Why did you do that?" "That was dumb." "You can't do anything right."

These thoughts are the heavily traveled path you've walked a million times. Your brain is just a computer. It simply matches past situations to present ones. So, it says, "You've used these lines in other embarrassing situations. I presume you want one or all of these again." It is trying to be helpful.

If you're going to change the "default message" you need to be prepared to forge a new path. If you can envision doing this in the woods, you know it takes work and effort. Creating a new path isn't easy but it has its rewards. So, when your brain automatically offers you snide, critical statements, you need to reject them and re-teach your brain what thoughts you DO want next time you're in an embarrassing situation. So, initially, when the critical thoughts pop up you will have to consciously stop and think something like, "Okay, this is just an accident, not the end of the world." or "This is inconvenient, not a tragedy." Your brain can be taught to pop up with non-judging, non-criticizing statements. You just have to do the work to teach it to realize the judgmental thoughts aren't needed any more.

The next step would be reinventing your inner voice into a loving supporter or coach. In difficult situations, try to imagine what words of encouragement your best friend or mentor would say to you. Or, if you were helping someone you loved through whatever it is you're dealing with at the moment, what would you say to them? Think of these positive statements and then say them to yourself often to encourage yourself and to celebrate how far you've come.

If you just took your first walk in therapy or you just did something you couldn't do before, train your inner voice to be congratulatory. Say the things to yourself that you would want to hear from others, such as: "Wow, that's great!" "Hey, great job!" You can be your own coach and you can encourage yourself rather than criticize yourself for being different.

REMEMBER:
- You choose your thoughts
- Ignore your inner critic and create an inner coach instead
- When you're feeling badly about trying a supportive device or service, ask yourself what a good coach would say
- Remove the "F" word from your vocabulary

Your thoughts:

_____

_____

_____

_____

_____

_____

_____

_____

_____

_____

_____

_____

_____

The world breaks everyone
and afterward many are strong
in the broken places.

Ernest Hemingway

Chapter 11

Feeling Fragile

After my trigeminal diagnosis, it took me quite a while to be able to label or identify what I was feeling because it was so new to me. Prior to my diagnosis, I was a bit of a bulldozer. I plowed ahead through each day, basically ignoring how I "felt" and just staying busy "doing" and working, etc. Since being diagnosed, and especially when my pain level is high, I'm tired, often edgy, and most everything feels too hard. I become startled easily, and I have fleeting waves of panic over silly and minor things. I often feel fragile, like one more thing might cause me to shatter into a million pieces.

I believe that feeling fragile is due to the depletion of our own inner resources and coping mechanisms. A new diagnosis, chronic pain, and new health complications are scary, yet we face them each day –actually day after day.

We face these challenges in the midst of loving our families, maintaining our jobs, paying bills, making dinner, maintaining friendships, etc. All the other parts of our lives don't stop just because we changed or are in pain. Life around us keeps going and we're doing our best to keep up. It may even feel tolerable until you realize the phone ringing or the dryer buzzing just scared the hell out of you, or made you want to scream or cry or hide. That's what I mean by feeling fragile. One more thing, no matter how small, feels like it will simply break you.

Think of a balloon that someone is blowing up. Every issue in your life gets two big puffs each. Start listing those issues as we did above. Everything good or bad gets two puffs: your significant other (two puffs), or not having a significant other if you're wanting one (two puffs), your kids, your grandkids, your job, money problems, bills, car repairs, housework, parents, friends –imagine how full that balloon is already! Now add two puffs each for chronic pain, doctors, attorneys, medications and their side effects, etc – by now the balloon is ready to burst if it hasn't already. (Thanks to B.G. for that analogy.)

Right before that balloon breaks the sides get so tight they almost vibrate. That's how tense we can get and that's why we feel fragile. Feeling fragile means we're depleted and we need to rest and replenish so we don't burst like that balloon.

Here are some things to consider trying to replenish or refuel yourself:

Counseling - Are you sick of me suggesting this? Good! Then try it. I have gone into counseling when I've felt fragile and I've never regretted it. Counseling can help you purge your emotional excess and help you learn new coping techniques.

Meditation - In the beginning you may want to use a guided meditation tape or CD to help you learn to sit quietly and calmly. It takes time to learn to quiet your mind but the benefits are well worth it. Meditation is rejuvenating.

Sleep - If pain or stress are interrupting your sleep, try napping when you can. I'm a proud napper. Napping on the weekend is how I reward myself for making it through the workweek. Read SARK's book on napping. It's fun.

Nutrition & Supplements - You must put decent fuel in for your body to keep functioning. Educate yourself on proper nutrition. Talk to your doctor about a good vitamin regimen to add to your routine.

Hobbies/Creativity - Every puff into that balloon was related to survival. We need to do more than survive. What brings out your passion? Try reading, writing, drawing, gardening – do something that makes your heart sing. I recently realized I wasn't doing enough to bring joy into my life. So I signed up for my first ever art/painting class. I'm doing something for the pure enjoyment of the experience.

Spirituality - Feed your spirit, as discussed earlier. Watch the sunset, listen to the rain, read poetry. Talk to God and the angels. They're waiting to hear from you.

Quiet time - When you're overwhelmed, give yourself some time to be quiet. Personally, when I'm in pain, loud noises and too much activity freaks me out. I need peace and quiet to gear up and steady myself for the next round of pain. If needed, take a sick day to rest and regroup.

Reward yourself - Remember being rewarded as a kid with a gold star, an allowance, or a treat? Do that for yourself. If you're in or have just come out of a stressful period, reward yourself. It doesn't have to be costly. You can reward yourself with a nap, a bubble bath, an hour at your favorite nature spot, a long drive in the country or your favorite type of ice cream cone.

For every one of these things you do for yourself regularly, you get to release one puff of air from that taut balloon called life.

It's hard to remember to do these things but they're important. The more you take care of yourself, the less fragile you'll feel.

REMEMBER:
- Feeling fragile means you need to pay extra attention to taking care of yourself
- Reward yourself
- Try starting a new hobby or pursuing a new interest

Your thoughts:

_____

_____

_____

_____

_____

_____

_____

_____

_____

_____

_____

Imagination is more important than Knowledge.

Einstein

I never spoke to God —
nor visited in Heaven ...
yet certain am I of the spot.

Emily Dickinson

Chapter 12

Doing It Differently
(and being ok with it)

We talked briefly about ignoring your inner critic and celebrating all of your accomplishments with your new challenge. Figuring out **how** to do it now is tough in itself. You need to be creative, develop strategies, accept failure at times, and try again. If you can't figure out how to do something, tell your doctor that you need a referral to a good occupational therapist. They have access to and knowledge about adaptive aids that can take the frustration out of many tasks.

As an example, there are "reachers" and "grabbers" that can help you pick up things. There are jigs that can stabilize things during food preparation if you are one handed. There are adaptive driving aids to get you back on the road – and on and on.

Remember the saying that there is nothing new under the sun? Well, it's true. Your disability is new to you. It's not new to the world, and that's good news! This means that others have lived, loved, and survived –even thrived with your similar disability. It's probable that there is an adaptation out there that can help you and lighten your burden.

If you're not ready for adaptations, that's ok. Just remember they're out there for you to investigate if and when you want to. Try to look at things creatively. If buttons are now hard for you, would it be possible to leave most of your shirt buttoned and just slip it over your head? I always had problems with the buttons on dress pants. Whenever I get a new pair, I have a seamstress sew the button on the front flap so it looks like it's always buttoned. Then on the inside, we put a hook and eye. Viola! Problem solved! Throw the rule book out the window and do what works.

Since I grew up with a mobility/coordination impairment, I was used to modifying things like clothing and activities. When I lived alone, I paid friends and neighbors for cleaning, snow removal, grass cutting and taking the garbage out. I could go grocery shopping, but I couldn't carry the groceries into the house. I always coordinated my shopping with a visit from family or friends, so they could carry everything in. It worked.

After developing the trigeminal pain, I lost strength slowly as my medication levels had to be increased. Because it was a slow decline, it was hard to know if I was getting worse or just having another bad day. As I began to fall more frequently for no reason, it gradually became apparent that my reality was changing. Of course, that meant that I had to change too.

I'm fortunate to have an understanding and helpful husband. He does most everything around the house because I'm pretty fatigued after work. I start work at 7 a.m. That means I leave by 6:30 a.m. In order to get ready for work and have 15 or 20 minutes to sit and let my legs regroup before I leave, I have to get up at 4 a.m. It's not because I spend forever primping. It's because my disability forces me to move slowly. I don't need help with my personal care routine. I just need time and lots of it.

Even if I have a day off and my husband doesn't, I get up with him anyway. Because of my knees buckling without warning, I feel it's safer to shower while he's home. So I get up earlier. I rearrange my life as needed for safety reasons. It's different than before, but this works too.

Plan ahead and be open to changing and doing things differently. Maybe you now need a stool to sit on for cooking or doing dishes. Would it help ease your burden to hire someone for lawn care? Part of handling your new disability means managing your energy and pain levels. Trying to ignore your limitations and do everything you did before you became disabled will only exhaust you. Modify the tasks that you can and ask for help for the things that can't be modified.

Another example of an easy problem solver: if you have weakness in your hands, keep a needle nose pliers handy. It's a great tool to help with everything from turning a key to unbuttoning stiff jean buttons. Buttons on jeans have been a problem for me. Now I take a steak knife and cut the button hole bigger. --Another quick and easy accommodation.

Stairs, even single steps like curbs can be difficult. Whenever possible I use the curb cut-out instead of stepping up the curb. My husband also modified the steps in our home. We had two large steps from the garage into the house. He built six three-inch steps for me instead, so that I could get in and out without struggling. Three-inch steps are a breeze, and again, a cheap modification.

Consider grab bars next to the toilet and in the shower. Just be sure they're anchored in a stud. There is no way to list even a fraction of the accommodations available to you. My point in discussing these few is to give you hope that what you need can probably be found or created. There **are** devices that can lighten your frustration.

REMEMBER:
- There is nothing new under the sun. Your disability is new to you, not to the experts
- Throw the rule book out and do what works as you approach new tasks. As corny as it sounds, it's true...where there's a will, there's a way!
- Consider adaptive aids when you're ready

Your thoughts:

_____

_____

_____

_____

_____

_____

_____

_____

_____

_____

The world is mud-luscious
and puddle-wonderful.

e.e. cummings

Keeping in touch with childhood memories
Keeps us believing in life's simple pleasures
like a rainy afternoon, a swingset, and
a giant puddle to play in.

Chapter 13

Watching For Miracles

I worked with an energetic healer who is quite gifted and has a wonderful outlook on life and the challenges we face. He helped me immensely during the time we worked together.

At one point we were talking about healing and miracles. He said that many people ask for miracles; they pray for healing but then fight the healing journey every step of the way. He said "I want to say to them, 'There are a hundred miracles that happen before your eyes every day and you don't see them. What makes you think you're going to see the healing miracle you're asking for when you don't open your eyes to see the others (miracles) happening in front of you every day?'"

That statement really made me think. I have done this…not purposefully, but I've done it. I have prayed for miracle healing. I've done releasing visualizations, affirmations, worked with energy healers, etc. I've even had some good results. My trigeminal pain has become much less frequent.

However, instead of validating the miracle of healing whether you consider it Divine Intervention or simply the body's ability to regenerate itself, I found myself fearing the next attack. Talk about a kill-joy!

I realized, when I analyzed my behavior, that I would get a knot in my stomach whenever I brushed my teeth, touched my cheek, or did anything else that caused the trigeminal pain to jump in the past. I wasn't affirming a miracle. I was affirming failure. I was appalled when I realized that my thoughts and fears were out of control and working against me.

It made no sense to me. I believe in healing, both the body's innate ability to heal and Divine healing. How and why would I sabotage my own healing process?

Part of the problem was not being fully aware, not paying close enough attention to how out of control my own fear was. The longer I went without pain, the more I feared that it was lurking right around the corner. But again, why was I anticipating the worst rather than believing that healing had occurred?

I have explored this ad nauseum alone and with friends. My theories may be helpful in your own pursuit of healing and miracles.

I have said to friends that I believe intermittent pain is similar to playing Russian Roulette or to living with an abusive person. You never know when or why it will strike. You never know how bad the episode will be or how long it will last. That uncertainty is crazy making. For the sake of your sanity, it starts to feel safer to anticipate the next attack, rather than to be caught off guard. And being caught off guard leads to what I consider to be the underlying fear which is, to me, disappointment.

That may sound trivial but consider this: Anyone with a disability has had to swallow a boatload of disappointment already. One of my (non-disabled) friends, in batting this around with me, said disappointment is not even an emotional descriptor that ever enters her mind. I doubt that most disabled people could say the same thing. We have had to deal with the disappointment of lost dreams, lost bodily functioning, lost jobs, etc. Many of us have faced these issues, dealt with them and kept going.

For me, I have accepted that my life is different now. It hasn't been easy but I've done it. And in doing this, in the process of coming to terms with what is, there is a sense of comfort or peace. So what happens to my comfort or peace if I dare to dream, dare to believe in miracles and then find out I'm wrong? What if I risk believing in healing and the pain comes back? Can I deal with the disappointment again? Can I accept this disability all over again? Is it better to stop believing and take what is now my reality and just live with it?

I have pondered all these questions. I have been digging in my brain ruthlessly for my own answers because what I believe in will influence any outcome from here on. Remember, knowledge is power. Once I realized that my thoughts were blocking my own healing, I had to decide <u>if</u> I was going to deal with this and <u>how</u>.

Dealing with this has been a process. I decided that I don't want to hold onto my disability just because it's safer to do that. I want to believe in healing for myself and for others. I want to clean the fear out of my thought systems. I want to progress as far as I can. The only way to do that is to release my fear and see where the road takes me.

I have been working with affirmations from Louise Hay's book *You Can Heal Your Life,* and have started to see some of my fear dissipate. I believe I'm on a healthier course now. I continue to believe in miracles. I continue to watch for them. I choose to see my pain-free days as gifts and I'm releasing my fear of future pain. When I become aware that I'm engaging in fear-based thinking, I busy my brain with healthy affirmations instead. My current affirmation is:

"I have completely released all negative thought patterns that created these conditions. I have fully released all fear, anger, guilt, resentment and pain. I now love and approve of myself completely. I am now able to communicate with ease, joy, love and grace. I am whole, healed, healthy, strong and safe."

Saying this calms my fears and reminds me that all is well.

I encourage you to look for miracles in your own life and your own healing journey. My advice is, don't give in to the luxury of fear. Fear constricts growth and healing. It forces you to stay stuck. And maybe you won't wake up one day, snap your fingers and have your old life back. Maybe your miracle will come in the form of lowered pain or a bit more energy or maybe your family will be a bit more helpful, or maybe the insurance company will stop arguing with you and finally pay that darned bill!! Whatever good comes your way, see it, acknowledge it, appreciate it and remain open to more good coming your way.

Try affirmations as a way of releasing fear. As suggested earlier, look deep within and try to determine where your fear stems from and then deal with that. Every step you take to release fear brings you closer to grace. It's worthy of your time and energy.

REMEMBER:
- Miracles happen every day. Start watching for them.
- Fear constricts your progress. Release your fear.
- Affirmations can calm the mind and retrain your thoughts to be more positive.

Your thoughts:

_____

_____

_____

_____

_____

_____

_____

_____

_____

_____

_____

_____

_____

_____

A friend is the one who comes in when the whole world has gone out.

grace Pulpit

Chapter 14

For Family and Friends

It was my initial plan to have multiple chapters just for family and friends. I thought about talking to you separately about counseling support, feeding your spirit and your own healing process. However, my feeling now is that doing this would be redundant. You likely need all the same love, support and gentle kindness that I recommend for the newly disabled person. You're suffering right along with them because you love them and because you can't take away their pain. Try to read as much of this as possible so that you can get an understanding of the issues your loved one is facing. You might also get some ideas for your own healing process.

Let's talk about some things that really are unique to family and friends of people who are disabled. You might feel guilt, awkwardness, fear, and a strong desire to take control of things "for their own good."

Feeling guilt is a strange and normal human emotion.

Whenever we see someone suffering or in pain, it's natural human kindness that makes us want to help. This is what is good and right in us! Sometimes, though, the next feeling, whether we become aware of it or not, is often guilt. Another person's sorrow or crisis forces us to re-evaluate our own life. We see all the good stuff we've taken for granted, like good health, steady employment, healthy family members, etc. All these things are blessings, and being grateful for them is positive. However, feeling guilty that you have these things when suddenly your friend or family member doesn't, is a waste of your energy.

You can't take away your loved one's pain or frustration. It is his/her journey. Be as supportive as you can be. But don't question or feel guilty about your own abundance. Look at this as hard, cold reality. If you were to acquire the same disability or lose everything you have, it wouldn't change your friend's situation one bit. Would it? You can't protect someone from their own experiences. Instead, turn your guilt into a more useful emotion -- appreciation! Our lives are so busy that we rarely take time to appreciate our blessings.

Use your new awareness of your blessings. Read your kids an extra story, take your dog for an extra walk, give your spouse an unexpected hug. Thank the Creator for your blessings. When appreciation is your dominant emotion your personality and coping abilities will have more elasticity. You'll find yourself being more tolerant and less angry. You'll be a much better support person when you're appreciative and grateful than when you're guilt ridden or angry.

Of course, in the beginning, there will be some awkwardness between you and your newly disabled loved one. This is normal and natural and you just have to give it time. Whenever there is a life changing event, relationships between people shift and change as we struggle to regain our balance. Remember when your best friends found their partner? They were less available, and the deck was reshuffled so to speak.

You didn't lose your friendship, but the relationship probably changed.

Now think about some other big events that you've gone through with friends and family like births, deaths, divorces, etc. Remember how the people involved changed? They were probably more uptight and less emotionally available. You were probably unsure of how to help or what to say in those situations too. –My advice is to let your newly disabled loved one know you care and ask if there is anything you can do. Do this often, because initially, the newly disabled person is going to be in a type of shock. They may not be able to tell you what they need, because they may not know themselves.

Further, in the beginning, it's going to be very painful for them to admit they need help. Be patient and give them time. It's not uncommon for newly disabled people to isolate themselves initially while they deal with shock and grief. Your gentle reminders that you can and want to help are important. Keep them coming.

It's also normal for newly disabled people to be crabby and impatient. Try to remember this has nothing to do with you. They are likely facing more fear than they've ever known. They are likely short-tempered because they're terrified. Give them some time.

I'm not, however, suggesting you tolerate any type of verbal or physical abuse, ever. If it gets to that point, remind them to see a counselor and be sure to take care of yourself first. I'm talking about non-threatening cranky behavior like: the coffee is too strong, the TV is too loud, the meatloaf is too salty, etc. This is irritating, but to be expected as the newly disabled person redefines their place in the world.

Again, if the behavior escalates and you feel threatened, contact your local domestic violence professionals for information and referral.

Perhaps some of the awkwardness is due to your lack of understanding of the situation. Your newly disabled loved one may not be talking about their situation because they're afraid of looking like a whiner. You're not asking because it's "impolite to pry." The result is that everyone feels weird because they're avoiding the big "it."

SO TALK ALREADY!

If you want to know the prognosis - ASK! If you want to know if they're in pain --ASK! Talking about real things shows you care. Otherwise, we risk the alternative, which is to be so concerned about decorum that we turn into very polite idiots! This is someone you care about! Talk about the hard things, so you both regain the balance of your relationship. It's okay to talk. It's okay to cry with them. It's okay to say you're afraid too. Some people keep all of their feelings quiet because they think they have to be strong for the other person. My opinion is that, if you're anything less than "real," you'll create a wedge or distance in your relationship.

I have friends and family who can't handle the hard stuff. When I've been flattened by a bout of pain, they avoid me. If they haven't been able to avoid me, they talk nervously and incessantly about inane things. I try to remember that they're doing the best they can. My desire is to ask them to be quiet, but, as my friend says, "If they knew better, they'd do better!" So I try not to add to their discomfort while trying to manage my own pain. Be a friend, not a nervous chatterbox. Maybe your loved one would like to talk or vent. Give them that opportunity.

Control is another issue that needs to be handled delicately. Many of us are "fix it" people. When someone is in crisis we jump in wanting to "fix" whatever happened. When the realization hits us that we can't fix the disability, the tendency might be to try to fix, manage, or control other aspects of the person's life. Avoid this behavior if you tend to be controlling.

Nothing good can come from usurping someone else's power. My suggestion is, "Ask – don't orchestrate." Ask if there are things that they want you to do. Suggest things you'd be willing to do. But don't presume to know what's best for another person. That is plain and simply obnoxious behavior. Before making these presumptions and acting on them, ask yourself if you'd want them treating you that way if the situation were reversed. Ah—that wouldn't be good, would it?

Don't judge other people's feelings either. Perhaps in your mind it appears that the person's emotions are counterproductive, and this may be true. However, telling someone not to feel what they're feeling won't change a thing except probably the nature of your relationship. They're already feeling overwhelmed, so telling them to "get over it" will only be insulting. You will quickly go from being a trusted someone to being a person to be avoided because you are adding to the problem. People hear judgment loud and clear. When one person presumes to tell another how to feel or to get over it, it feels like an attack. It is NOT helpful. It's easy to hear judgment or "the loaded gun" in your voice.

I've had friends and family who have felt amazingly free to dish out all kinds of unsolicited advice. If it's given gently, I may engage in a conversation with them because sometimes these things can be "teachable moments," meaning maybe we can both learn something.

However, if I hear "the loaded gun" in their voice, the one that suggests I'm clearly an idiot, and they obviously know what's best, the conversation is over. I'm more forgiving when it involves family. For the sake of maintaining family ties, I will tolerate more and forgive more. However, I have ended friendships for this kind of behavior. I will still forgive them in my heart. However, I simply won't subject myself to their judgment/loaded gun. Do not presume to know what's best for another person.

If you are truly concerned about your disabled loved one, then show concern not judgment. Tell the person you care and what you're worried about and why. Ask if they're aware of the issue, and if you can help them with it. If they're not ready to address it, then let it go and don't badger them. Nature/God/Universal Wisdom may help them to move through it in a different way.

Years ago I spoke to a group of people about these issues because their co-worker was newly disabled, and they wanted to know how to behave now. I gave them a lot of credit for trying to understand and knowing they had a lot to learn. One participant voiced a concern about the person being suicidal. Another person jokingly suggested they simply block the wheelchair ramp, so the person couldn't leave work and hurt themselves.

My response was "not funny." I also told the person not to make insulting jokes like that around me or any other disabled person. It is certainly possible that a totally healthy person has no idea how delicate the balance is for someone with a disability. I depend on crutches. Without them I don't walk. That's damned scary. In college someone stole them. I couldn't get to class that day.

Many disabled adults rely on some kind of adaptation or another. Without these adaptations, (like crutches or fully charged wheelchair batteries or hearing aid batteries) life comes to a standstill. People with disabilities are painfully aware of this fragile balance while others haven't a clue. Joking about blocking the wheelchair ramp only adds to feelings of vulnerability. Don't be that cruel.

At that meeting, I suggested the person who was closest in friendship ask the newly disabled person if there was a risk of suicide. If there was, then the doctor treating the person needed to be made aware of the problem. If the person was in more immediate danger, the police are always an option. This is what you'd do for anyone who was suicidal. Hindering their mobility just because you can is a direct assault on their dignity. Don't do it!

Throughout this chapter I've made some bold statements regarding what to do and not to do for your newly disabled loved one. What about you? If you live in the same house, then your world is just as upset as theirs. Immediate family is hit the hardest. Other people can visit, be supportive, and then go back to their own lives. This, however, **is** your life.

My suggestion is that you consider all of the healing suggestions in this book for yourself as well as your loved one. Talk about the big "it," feed your spirit, take naps, take long baths, meditate, eat decently and above all, be kind to yourself. You will be grieving too. Find a good counselor for yourself so that you can be supported through all of the changes that come with disability.

REMEMBER:

- When you're wondering about this new situation ASK!!!
- Awkwardness is normal. You'll get through it
- Avoid judgmental and controlling behavior
- Take care of yourself

Your thoughts:

_____

_____

_____

_____

_____

_____

_____

_____

_____

_____

_____

_____

_____

Sometimes the most important thing
in a whole day is the rest we take
in between two deep breaths.

Etty Hillesum

Let the winds of enthusiasm sweep through you. Live life with gusto.

Dale Carnegie

Chapter 15

Going Beyond

Through all of this, we have been talking about how to get through the hard stuff, the pain, both physical and emotional. Healing is a process. It is on-going. It's not like a trip to the mall to buy something. Some might think, "Okay, I'm going to do these exercises or read these books and everything will be fine again." Don't be surprised if your healing journey is more complex than that. Good days and bad days will continue. Hopefully, if you continue on your healing path, the good days will start to outnumber the bad.

One way to move toward better days is to start to go beyond the scope of your disability and "give back". It's easy to become self absorbed while you're in the adjustment process. Some of this is natural and necessary. It stands to reason that you need to focus on the issue in order to understand it and heal it. Don't feel badly when you need to focus on healing. Healing is a learned process of taking care of yourself. It's just like learning to drive a car. You had to read about the requirements and then practice them. You couldn't have any passengers until you were skilled enough to drive safely.

Healing is similar to this. You've got to make time for it and then apply what you've learned. Once you regain your equilibrium you may want to consider taking on "passengers" or doing something for others. Helping others is a great way to take your mind off of your own stuff. It gets you to start to focus on other issues besides your own. It also allows you to start regaining self-esteem because it helps you to feel useful and productive.

You don't need to go overboard. Start with small things with shorter time commitments, such as visiting an elderly friend who may not be able to get out often, volunteering to help with an activity sponsored by your support group, calling someone who is going through a tough time and being supportive of them – **listen** to their stuff instead of talking about yours. Monitor how you feel before and after you do something kind for someone else. I believe you'll find that you feel more upbeat when you "give back."

As your stamina and confidence improve you can increase the types of things you engage in, such as helping with your local literacy council, Big Brothers-Big Sisters, etc. Commit yourself and your time very gradually so you'll still have time to take care of yourself.

You've probably heard the expression "what goes around comes around." I think the more common interpretation of this is somewhat negative, meaning that there are consequences for bad behavior. I believe though that it can also mean that good things come as a result of positive or helping behavior. – Helping someone else can also be helping and uplifting for you. Give it a whirl and see what you think.

I also believe that it is a way of enlarging and continuing the circle of support. Remember the movie "Pay It Forward"? If you haven't seen it, I suggest you rent it. It is a lovely, heartwarming story of a boy who, instead of paying someone back for a good deed, decides to pay it forward. He does something nice for 3 people with the understanding that they will then pay it forward to 3 more people. Of course, good grows exponentially from this. Really, see the movie.

Your helpful acts are similar to this. Helping someone else is a way to show gratitude for the help you received when you were in crisis. If you didn't receive the help you needed through your crisis then helping others might be a nice way of ensuring that someone else doesn't have to go it alone as you did. It may then result in creating a better support system so you don't feel so alone in the future.

REMEMBER:
- What goes around comes around
- Random acts of kindness help all involved to feel better about today
- Helping others may also help you feel more connected

Your thoughts:

_____

_____

_____

_____

_____

_____

_____

_____

_____

_____

_____

_____

_____

THINGS TO REMEMBER
AS YOU GO THROUGH YOUR JOURNEY.....

- Be kind to yourself

- Look for reasons to celebrate what you've done and what you're doing

- Talk about "IT"

- Ask for help

- Feed your Spirit

- Take a nap

- Be open to doing things differently than before

- Plan ahead and be safe

- Meditate, relax

- Get out and give back

- Trust in higher wisdom, look for the learning and teaching opportunities

- Be patient with yourself and with loved ones, you're all learning a new way of life

- There is wisdom in taking it "one day at a time"

May your eyes continue to see beautiful
and significant things, and your soul
dance to good music.

Chapter 16

My Wish for You

As I put the final touches on this book I am both happy at the thought of its completion and a bit sad because it feels like letting go, and that is never easy for me. I am concerned that I may have forgotten something or not explained something clearly enough. However, I've come to the conclusion that this process, like everything else in life, is a matter of trust. I have to trust that what is within these pages is enough for now. I have to trust that it will be useful to some of you. I simply have to trust that Universal Wisdom guided this process and will carry it through to its proper place.

My wish for you is that you are able to regain trust in your life and in Universal Wisdom. I hope that you can find it in yourself to grieve your loss or disability, acknowledge that life is changed and eventually realize that you can create something beautiful as you are now. Remember, there is life after disability and it doesn't have to suck!

Keep that tree story in mind and try to grow with your disability. Accept it within yourself as the tree did and keep growing. Continue to love, laugh, learn, grow, and create. Watch for miracles. Continue to give back. The world needs you and your unique gifts.

Consider opening yourself to Divine Guidance. There is Wisdom available to us all if we open to it.

I wish for you to have a healing journey full of support and love. Trust that in time, life will teach you what you need to know and that Universal Wisdom is guiding you too.

Be well,

Dinah

RECOMMENDED AUTHORS

So many beautiful and conscious people have put themselves out there for us and given us words to heal by. These are the authors who helped me in my healing journey. They may help you too. I'm not suggesting specific books because what speaks to you may be different than what helped me. Try doing a web search for their titles. See what jumps out at you and trust that it is the next brick on your healing path.

Louise Hay - She healed herself of cancer. She has developed healing meditations/journeys for others. I heard her speak in person. She is a gift to this world.

Florence Scovel-Schinn - She believed in the power of your words to create your reality. Her work is simply profound.

Sondra Ray - She has excellent advice on healing yourself and your relationships.

Don Miguel Ruiz - He is amazing. His work suggests adhering to four basic principles as a way of growing and healing. He is a prayerful, spiritual teacher.

SARK - Oh, she is a joy and a "MUST READ." Her titles are fun. Her books give you a broad smile because they are playful and joyful. They are in color and have lots of artwork. When you need a smile, a hug, a nap or a profound thought to ponder, you'll find it in her books.

Chrissy Ogden Marsh - All of the inspirational photographs and quotes are courtesy of Chrissy Ogden Marsh. They are from her exquisite card line "Bonair Daydreams". To access her card line you can visit her on the web at www.bonairdaydreams.com or toll free 1-888-2-BONAIR

INVITATION

Please visit our website at www.chasing-normal.com

We would love to hear from you.

We're developing new tools for supporting people with disabilities and rehab professionals. Check back with us periodically to see if we can continue to be of assistance to you on your journey.

If you found this book and/or website helpful, consider inviting Dinah to speak to your group about surviving and thriving with disability. There's no end to what creative intent can arrange.

Let's stay connected and enjoy the journey, remembering that all the "some days" we've been waiting for are built by every one of our "todays". Let's make every today something to be happy about!

NOTES